Endorsements

This book relates the journey of a woman who just tries to hear the heart of God with a group of kids. And the incredible begins! Together they are launched in a new chapter of the book of Acts, discovering a thread in the history of their nation that God is unveiling for an end-time purpose. Along the way they discover that God has been sharing the same thoughts with others in Canada, and a closer walk between the generations emerges. Just dig into the book and see how the Lord takes pleasure in revealing His wisdom and power in a company of people with a burning heart for Him.

~Alain Caron
Pastor of Le Chemain, and Senior Leader with Watchmen for the Nations

We of the "more mature" generations tend to think that ministry should be in our hands, that young people are nice to have around but lack credibility. Carolin Sadler was armed with the belief that children really have something to say about and contribute to the advancement of God's Kingdom, even on the world stage. She has, in this book, mapped out her journey with a bunch of normal, average kids who learned how to walk the walk, hear God's voice for themselves and go into situations that many of us older ones would have been afraid to go into. This is a chronicle of faith—the sort of faith we should all walk in.

~Peter Jordan
YWAM International Leader

These children have been on an incredible journey and it has been a delight to watch it unfold. The prophet Joel told us that, in the last days, God would pour His Spirit on our sons and daughters. Truly this has happened as these young people have heard, seen and prophesied through visions and dreams what the Lord is saying to the church today. They have often gone before the adults with amazing accuracy, both locally in Manitoba and nationally in Canada, in the prayer initiatives that we have been led to do. May the Lord bless all who read this book with delight in His wisdom and counsel.

~Ruth Wall
Coordinator, City-wide prayer and
March for Jesus, Winnipeg.

The Journey is a delightful story that will leave you with a firm conviction that God can and does use children as easily as (and sometimes more than) he does adults. It is a testimony to the fact that children don't have a "junior Holy Spirit" and being young in years is no hindrance to God. Carolin's account of her journey with the King's Kids will inspire you, build your faith and remind you that, "unless we all become as a little child..." I highly recommend it!

~Sara Maynard
Founder & Director,
Cityscape Prayer Ministries

The Journey

Following The Rainbow

All around him was a glowing halo, like a rainbow shining in the clouds on a rainy day. This is what the glory of the Lord looked like to me. When I saw it, I fell face down on the ground...

Ezekiel 1:28 (NLT)

The Journey

Following The Rainbow

Carolin Sadler

The Journey...Following the Rainbow
Copyright © 2008 Carolin Sadler

ISBN-10: 1-897373-43-0
ISBN-13: 978- 1-897373-43-9

All rights Reserved. No part of this publication may be reproduced, stored in a retrieval system or transmitted in any form or by any means—electronic, mechanical, photocopy, recording or any other—except for brief quotations imprinted reviews, without the prior permission of the author.

Unless otherwise noted, all scripture quotations are from the *New American Standard Bible*, copyright © The Lockman Foundation 1960, 1962, 1963, 1971, 1973, 1995; International Bible Society, All rights reserved

Scripture quotations marked "TLB" are taken from *The Living Bible* Copyright ©1971 by Tyndale House publishers, Wheaton Illinois 60187, All rights reserved.

Scripture quotations marked "NIV" are taken from *The Holy Bible, New International Version* © 1973, 1978, 1984, by International Bible Society, All rights reserved.

Scripture quotations marked "NLT" are taken from the Holy Bible, New Living Translation, copyright 1996, 2004. Used by permission of Tyndale House Publishers, Inc., Wheaton, Illinois 60189. All rights reserved.

Printed by Word Alive Press
131 Cordite Road, Winnipeg, MB R3W 1S1
www.wordalivepress.ca

This story is dedicated to all the kids, leaders and friends who have walked together to make this story possible. They have selflessly given of their time, finances and energy to follow God's direction step by step.

But especially, this is dedicated to my family, who patiently stood by me and helped to figure out "the journey."

Table of Contents

SECTION ONE

Chapter 1	~ A New Way of Thinking	3
Chapter 2	~ Baby Steps	9
Chapter 3	~ Step by Step You'll Lead Me	17
Chapter 4	~ Do Not Despise the Day of Small Beginnings	27

SECTION TWO

Chapter 5	~ Start of Daniel Prayer Groups	39
Chapter 6	~ Quebec: Pulling a Team Together	43
Chapter 7	~ Brownsburg	53
Chapter 8	~ Why Montreal?	61
Chapter 9	~ Light Be!	71

SECTION THREE

Chapter 10	~ Apples and Direction	83
Chapter 11	~ Next Steps	93
Chapter 12	~ Gathering the Team	103
Chapter 13	~ Israel	117
Chapter 14	~ Stones Laid Down . . . and Removed	133

SECTION FOUR

Chapter 15	~ Hand in Hand	151
Epilogue		163
Photo Gallery		167

SECTION FIVE

Activation	
A) Waiting on the Lord/ Hearing God's Voice	179
B) Putting on the "Rainbow Coat"	184
Postscript	193
Endnotes	195

Section One

*Bring My sons from afar
and My daughters from the ends of the earth...*

So that you may know and believe Me...

So you are My witnesses...

Isaiah 43:6b, 10b, 12b

Chapter 1

A New Way of Thinking

It was the first day of boot camp: July 2nd, 1996. The team was excited about the prospect of going to Target World, a worldwide King's Kids conference in Atlanta, and then on to Mexico. Everyone was milling around and checking each other out, especially the new kids that had just come from out of town. What was in store? I had never led a team before and I felt totally out of my element just preparing for the outreach this far. But what an adventure we were about to embark on! If I felt unqualified before, the events that happened the first few days would certainly confirm it.

The journey really started the year before. A King's Kids team came to Winnipeg as part of the mid-decade (1995) Vision 2000 initiative in Canada. They met at a church downtown and prepared a presentation that would challenge us to reach out in our communities.

However, what stuck out for me was the exuberance and sincerity of the kids that presented. The worship dances they had prepared were unlike any I had ever seen before and I felt the presence of God come into the room. I was moved to tears and immediately longed for our family and other kids to be involved in this type of ministry. I had never seen or imagined that kids could so effectively and powerfully minister with authority.

After the meeting finished, I asked around to see who I should speak with to ask about the ministry of King's Kids. They directed me to Russell Sanche, but he wasn't around, having gone to Tim Horton's for coffee with some of the young people. Not to be deterred, I followed him down the street to Tim Horton's and accosted him with, "Can you tell me about King's Kids and how I could be involved?"

Now, when I get an idea in my head I can be direct and forget about minor details, like...introductions. You see, Russell didn't know me from Adam, and he gave me a bewildered look that said, "Great, but WHO are you and how did you find me? I am enjoying my coffee." Well, the long and the short of it was that, after he realized that I was serious and maybe not so crazy after all, he told me about an initial training weekend, "the Generation of Destiny," that would be held in Winnipeg a few months later.

During this time my daughter was involved in a sacred dance class that met at the church where the training weekend was to be held. She was learning a song by Rich Mullins called "Sometimes by Step."[1]

Chapter 1 ~ A New Way of Thinking

The words that leapt out over and over again were: *"Step by step You'll lead me, and I will follow You all of my days."* These words were with me when I woke up and when I went to sleep. Where was God leading us and why was He highlighting this to me at this time?

My husband, Doug, was the pastor of a church and there we led a kid's worship team that involved my children and a few of their friends from Sunday school. So why not combine the dance and the worship team and offer to help lead worship at one of the training sessions? This was gratefully accepted, and as we prepared, something powerful emerged that brought tears to many eyes. God was at work and we knew that there was a special anointing on that song as it was presented. *"Oh God, you are my God. I will ever praise you, seek you in the morning, and learn to walk in your ways..."*

During the weekend seminar, truths were presented that I had heard before but had not thought of as pertaining to kids in ministry. I learned that King's Kids is a ministry of Youth with a Mission, committed to leading children and youth of all nations to a proven knowledge of God and making Jesus Christ known to all peoples. Foundational to the ministry is the thought that God has called children to be worshippers first, and as such, all ministry flows out of a heart of worship with a desire to bring joy to God's heart.

Children have the same Holy Spirit as adults do. Children can hear God's voice and minister unto Him.

Section One

God anointed many children in the Bible to do radical things for Him such as: Samuel, Daniel, Josiah, Esther, Mary and MANY more. Why not the Shawn's, Josh's, Amanda's of today? I was also confronted with the urgency of the times and could not get away from it.

The seminar leaders pointed out that there were two other times in Biblical history that were similar to today. Satan understood the times and recognized that God was ready to fulfill His promises by sending a deliverer. So he set out to abort God's purposes and launched an attack to destroy the babies born at that time to prevent God's representative from reaching maturity.

The deliverer in each case was a threat to the kingdom of darkness because through his obedience and faithfulness it would be pushed back. The first "deliverer" was Moses, who was sent to deliver the children of Egypt from bondage and through whom God gave the Law and the nation of Israel was formed. The second was Jesus, through whom salvation for the world was secured and the church was birthed. During those times God also established new ways for mankind to have greater relationship with Him.

The time today is different, as it seems as if the enemy is trying to *eliminate a whole generation*. If he cannot abort a "baby in the womb," then he will try to abort the baby's calling and destiny in whatever way he can.[2] If he cannot kill, he will make sure the life is wasted. It doesn't take much to realize that there is an all-out assault against this young generation today.

Chapter 1 ~ A New Way of Thinking

So what can we do? We are at a crossroads in history. Throughout church history there have been crossroads where children and young adults were used to introduce an entire generation to the manifestation of God's Spirit.[3] We must mobilize to meet the challenge and call for the truest form of Christianity, filled with God's Spirit and Power. That is the only answer we can offer to win this generation.[4]

What you believe children are capable of spiritually will directly affect your expectation of them and where you will be able to lead them. Our primary goal in teaching the children is to help them to *know* God, not only with head knowledge, but with heart knowledge. Our responsibility is to train them to live a lifestyle of worship. This leads to another foundational principal—the principal of the generations walking together.

> *Catherine Brown a prophet from England, shares in a word from the Lord:*
> *"The children will require to be mentored in like manner as Eli mentored Samuel in order that they can be trained to discern My voice for themselves, and respond to Me in obedience, for it is My desire that none of their words will fall to the ground. There is a need for this generation to be nurtured and discipled."*

Over the next few months I just "happened" to read various articles and attend meetings that confirmed what the Lord seemed to be telling me. "Let the little children come to me, and do not hinder them, for the kingdom of God belongs to such as these."[5] The Lord has not changed. It is still His desire to have the children brought close to Him.

Every part of the body is important. Likewise, children are the little members of the church, and they are necessary for the well-being of the whole church.[6] It is not just our ministry to them, but also *their ministry to us* that must be considered. WE NEED THEM! We need the little members to be released to be all that the Lord wants them to be. Many children are several years old spiritually and have no ministry. The mentality of the church has been simply to prepare them for "someday when they grow up" when, in fact, they are well able to minister in many different ways right now.[7]

An article in *Christian Week* entitled, "Do not hinder the children," further confirmed what the Lord was telling me. In it Esther Illinsky states, "A new breed of children—righteous seed—who are destined to fulfill God's eternal plans and purposes is emerging. They are being nurtured, trained and equipped for this hour and will rise up as a mighty prayer force—to petition God on behalf of their generation and in the mighty name of Jesus, to silence the enemy."[8]

Chapter 2

Baby Steps

I WAS FINALLY getting the picture.

"But Lord, what do You want me, us, as a family to do about this? Where are You leading us?"

A barrage of songs crossed our path: "God is in control"; "Be not afraid I go before you always, come follow me and I will give you rest"; "Father of creation raise up a chosen generation"; "This is no time for fear, this is the time for faith and determination"; "Though there be giants in the land I will not be afraid." These lyrics became our heart's cry and prayer.

A while later, I was prompted to call Russell Sanche and ask, "Is there another King's Kids outreach going soon that we could be involved with?" My idea was that we could come and serve on a team, he would organize and lead it, I would cook and maybe Doug could take his vacation and drive or whatever…lead worship…he's good at that. Well, Russell said he would get back to me. A few days later, he called back and told us about a worldwide King's Kids mission's conference called "Target World" taking place the following summer in Atlanta, Georgia. This being a global conference meant that kids from many nations of the world would be attending. Following the conference, the kids would fan out to both North and South America on outreach, and the designation for the team from Central Canada was Mexico. The scripture that the Lord led the Global King's Kids leaders to was, *"Bring My sons from afar, My daughters from the ends of the earth...that you might know and believe Me...and be My witnesses."*[9] The time frame would be from July 2–July 27.

"Would you be interested?" he asked.

I immediately responded, "YES!"

"Good," he replied. "You can lead the team from Winnipeg."

Sputter, gasp, WHAT?

"I thought that we could join you guys and just come along." I replied. SILENCE...Man, was that a long silence!

"Well, we were praying and we think you are supposed to lead the team. Get back to me after you have prayed about it."

What could I say? "Okay," I whispered, not at all convinced.

Although it wasn't what I was comfortable with at the time, Doug encouraged me, "Call back and ask him what is involved. That's where you start. You can do it. If it is from God, He will help you."

Chapter 2 ~ Baby Steps

So I called back, reluctant but determined. I found out that the Winnipeg team was to be a part of a larger team from Calgary and Thunder Bay. We would each do our own training and then rendezvous in Atlanta. I would have to organize the training for Winnipeg. I also found out that the cost was going to be about $2300 per person. I quickly calculated and realized that it would be $9200 for four of our family to go! If I was overwhelmed before, I was panicking now. "WHAT have I gotten myself into? But yes, Lord...step by step You'll lead me and I will follow You all of my days." It was the beginning of some of the most exciting times of my life.

I managed to get in touch with Doug and Jeanie Halstead, a couple Russell mentioned who had been involved with King's Kids in the past in Winnipeg. I was told their daughter, Sarah, had a FOUR-inch thick red binder with all the training material I needed to lead a team. I laughed. How was I going to find the time to read this thing and implement it? I was still a pastor's wife and had three young children.

A week later, when I was picking my kids up from school, I ran into the mother of one of their friends. She was going to work and I was just making small talk, asking her what she did. She mentioned that she was an administrator involved in coordinating the home care for an elderly gentleman. As she shared what she did, she stopped and asked, "By the way, you don't happen to have some nursing skills, do you?" I told her that I had trained as a nurse way back but had let my registration lapse. She replied, "Well, would you be interested in picking up a few shifts at Dr. Mac's house? You don't have to have current registration, as you would work as a Health Care Aide." I could not believe my ears. I had been praying about how in the world we could come up with the funds for the outreach, and here I was being offered a job. The time fit in nicely with everything else I had to do as well, so off I went to "work" for the first time in fourteen years and cared for this lovely gentleman…who slept most of the time. Guess where I read and studied this HUGE red binder? To boot, the money earned there was just enough!

So the ball was rolling. But now the team. Where would I find kids for the team? And leaders? As I read the manual, I realized I needed people who could carry specific roles and a ratio of one adult for three kids. If Doug and I both went we could take six kids. Whew, well that was a start! As I busied myself trying to pull this all together (stressing out, as one of my kids so kindly informed me), the Lord quietly impressed on me to rest, for He would bring the team together. My role was to be alert and to follow His promptings as to who to ask. Taking this new posture, over the next while as we approached first one and then another, amazingly, eight kids were interested and another adult expressed interest as well. There was only one other person who frequently came to mind. However, I had no idea who she was or how to get a hold of her. She had sung at a school assembly a year ago; that was all I knew about her.

Chapter 2 ~ Baby Steps

One Saturday in late winter, we decided to bring everyone together to get to know one another and to pray. A big snowstorm had hit the city the night before and the snowploughs had been out and the day was beautiful—everything was covered and sparkling with a soft blanket of snow. By afternoon we were sitting on pins and needles waiting for everyone to come. One...then two arrived...a while later, the third. The trickle stopped. What was going on? Okay, it had snowed, but this was Winnipeg and we're used to a "bit" of snow. Thirty minutes later, the fourth arrived; she had driven past our house three times and couldn't see it, even though it isn't an obscure house. Then Holly called to let us know she was driving in from out of town and was stuck in a snow drift. Sarah called that they would be late as they had locked their key in the car after shovelling it out of the snow and her husband was going to the dealership to get another key. They never did make it, because after he got the key, he forgot to unlock the door and locked the second key in the trunk. Ouch!

By this time we figured that "someone" was not too happy about this get-together and we started praying for real. Almost immediately, the phone rang and someone asked, "Is there a meeting for King's Kids today?"

I replied hesitantly, "...Yes."

"Well, my daughter heard about it and wondered if she could come and check it out?" I felt a bit put on the spot, but thought Why not? We had been praying.

Section One

On the heels of the phone call, the doorbell rang and another person came in. He said, "Sorry I'm late, but we were in a car accident on the way! We're okay but the car is a bit dented." The door opened again about ten minutes later, and I couldn't believe it. Here stood the girl that had been on my mind that I couldn't find—Kathleen. She was the one whose mom had just called. GOD IS IN CONTROL!

As we shared, God's presence flooded the room, and what was to have been a short get-together turned into a four-hour prayer meeting. The chilli dried out, but that was a small price to pay for how God's Spirit burned in our hearts that evening.

Over the next few months, the Lord brought three more people from out of town to join us for a total of fourteen on the team. Many lessons in God's provision were learned by all of us.

At the Atlanta Airport eleven-year-old Amanda was playing with the buttons on an ATM bank machine. Much to her surprise, it spat out a $50 bill. We gathered around her and suggested she try to return it to the bank, but the bank teller told her that there was no record of the transaction and as far as they were concerned it was hers. The Lord had just finished providing miraculously for her and her mom. A day before we were to leave, they were $1,200 short—$700 for outreach costs and $500 for her rent—and therefore, they would not be able to leave. As a team we had prayed and still they were short, even after money had been coming in. That evening Amanda's mom thought, "I'll go check my bank one

Chapter 2 ~ Baby Steps

last time." To her AMAZEMENT, someone had deposited into her account enough money to cover not only the $650, but also the rent for her apartment! When Amanda received the $50, we all recognized that God is an extravagant God. We already knew He could take care of our needs, but He also wanted a young girl to have some spending money...just for fun.

Chapter 3

Step by Step You'll Lead Me

Now, back to boot camp: July 2nd, 1996, in the basement of Ness Ave. Baptist Church where Doug was pastor. The church had graciously opened the building to us. After introductions, get to know you games and a time of worship, we settled in for a good meal that some of the ladies of the church had provided. We formed our "action groups," had devotions together and then settled in for the evening on mats and sleeping bags—girls downstairs, boys upstairs. ("Action groups" are small accountability groups within the larger team led by some of the older teens. They are, in turn, responsible for clean up, fun activities and so on.)

The next day, I was equipped with my trusty red binder and scads of notes. I wanted very much to "do it right" and was going to rely heavily on this wealth of information. Number one...start with exercise. So okay,

Kathleen took the kids out for a jog around the block and some callisthenics to wake everyone up. Breakfast, and then worship, followed by a time of waiting on the Lord and a speaker to help prepare our hearts for the outreach. The kids were getting along just great and it was all running smoothly. Whew...we can do this!

But God had another idea. I had verbalized that I wanted the Lord to lead us step by step, and He had taken me at my word. During boot camp, some time was spent as a team "waiting on the Lord." This was where we asked God to show us what was on His heart for the outreach and for our lives.

The steps included a time of worship, where we focused on praising God for who He is, then a time of confession, asking God to deal with any unconfessed sin or resentment. We then acknowledged that we cannot pray effectively without the help of the Holy Spirit and asked Him to guide and control our thoughts. One of the leaders rebuked any thoughts or intents of the enemy in the name of Jesus. We surrendered our own imagination and burdens to the Lord, and with thankfulness, we waited silently for Him to speak. (A more detailed version of these steps is in the Activation section at the end of this book.)

I was unprepared for the thoughts that the Lord shared with us. Little did we know that the thoughts and prayer pictures that the Lord showed us that day and during subsequent days were to be blueprints for what we would be walking out for the next twelve years! As the story unfolds I will draw you back to what the Lord highlighted during this time.

Chapter 3 ~ Step by Step You'll Lead Me

The first time, Kristy-Anne, or Kitty, as we sometimes called her, saw a prayer picture of a large bowl of multicoloured liquid in the sky. Then she saw the bowl tipping and it started to rain rainbow colours. The next day she saw a large dark brown wall. The wall was so huge that that we couldn't get around it or over it. There was only one thing left to do, and that was to say the Lord's Prayer: "Thy kingdom come thy will be done on earth as it is in heaven!" When we did this, a hammer came down from heaven with a flash of light and the wall came down.

Shortly afterwards, our speaker, Doug Halstead, came in and said, "What we are going to talk about today is reconciliation. It is so important not to have walls between us, especially as we think of going to Atlanta, where so many different nations of the world are going to be gathered. So let us start by saying the Lord's Prayer and asking that ONLY God's will would be done."

Kitty's mouth dropped open and we all got very quiet. Because Doug had not been with us during our prayer time, he had no idea of what had been shared. As he spoke about the need for reconciliation and how we stereotype people, a number of the team members started to cry. The children verbalized many walls of hurt and it became a time of healing as the kids prayed for each other and the hurts of other people groups.

Johnathan shared how over the previous few days the phrase "Jesus wept" kept coming to his mind over and over again. He now felt that God had spoken to him that He wept at the pain that he had inside. Just as Jesus wept at Johnathan's pain, His heart was moved with compassion for the pain in our cities. Afterwards Johnathan cried and cried. Some of the leaders prayed over him and he was immediately delivered from fears and rejections that he had been carrying for months. He was subsequently FILLED with incredible joy, after which he lay seemingly asleep for a long time. When he came to, he shared how he had a dream of a turntable with a diamond ring on it. This newfound joy remained with him throughout the outreach.

All these visions and experiences were TOTALLY outside my comfort zone. I had read that God speaks to kids—after all, we have all read the story of Samuel's "Speak, for Your servant is listening!"[10] But could it be possible that God would share His heart for a nation with a group of kids in the basement of a church? Over the next few years we discovered that yes, He had, and He would continue to do so.

The picture of walls was seen again in Atlanta by a few members of the team. One of them saw a picture of many walls in a row—twelve of them. In the vision we tried to climb over the first wall, but again, it was too large. Then we all shouted the name of Jesus and the wall came down. We climbed over the rubble and came up to another wall. Other people joined us. Again we tried to climb over the wall and couldn't. When we shouted the name of Jesus it, too, came down. This we did twelve times until all the walls were down.

Chapter 3 ~ Step by Step You'll Lead Me

And it shall come to pass afterward, that I will pour out my spirit on all flesh; and your sons and your daughters shall prophesy, your old men shall dream dreams, your young men shall see visions: (Joel 2:28 KJV)

~

In Atlanta there was a prayer tent that was overseen by Paul Hawkins, a teacher focusing on intercession and spiritual warfare in YWAM. Early on in our time there, he approached our team and asked if we could spend some time in the prayer tent. He mentioned that he felt we had a call to pray for Canada and for reconciliation. He had no idea what God had been speaking to the kids at boot camp. But we were also not aware at that time of the need for reconciliation in Canada. So, in our spare time, the team would go into the prayer tent.

One afternoon there was a time of prayer focusing on praying for the various provinces and people groups in Canada. Once again, God's presence came as the kids prayed for hurts between the provinces to be healed and especially for the walls surrounding the First Nations people to come down. James, a thirteen-year-old Métis on the team, stood on stage and, weeping, sang and called out for walls of misunderstanding and prejudice to be broken down. "We will break dividing walls; we will break dividing walls in the name of the Lord!" Little did we know, that very week his father was in dialogue with a Mennonite congregation to purchase their church building for a work to reach the Aboriginal people in the heart of Winnipeg. They had proposed a purchase price of $100,000. However, there was no way a fledgling inner-city work could afford that, even though it was a generous offer. A few weeks later, the Mennonite congregation came back and, after prayer, decided to GIVE the building to this new work.

Let Your Glory Fall

Just prior to boot camp, we were seeking the Lord as to what kind of team this should be. In King's Kids there are performing arts teams, service teams, intercession teams and sports teams. "How do YOU, Lord, want to equip and prepare this team?"

As we looked at the kids that were to be a part of the team and thought about what we would be doing in Atlanta and in Mexico, the Lord impressed on us that this was a "performing arts" team. So what would we prepare? Very clearly, He impressed on us that we were to focus on worship. He then went out of His way to highlight the songs and the people to choreograph the music and teach the kids. The same lady, Esther, who had taught the dance to Rich Mullins' "Sometimes by Step" that was presented at the Generation of Destiny seminar, invited me to come over to hear David Ruis' song, "Let Your Glory Fall."[11] I had not heard it before, but immediately my spirit leapt at the words. "Yes, Lord, raise up a generation that will march through the land declaring Your praises! Let Your glory FILL the earth!"

Chapter 3 ~ Step by Step You'll Lead Me

However, as the kids were learning the dance during boot camp the girl's choreography clicked beautifully but I just didn't feel good about the boy's part. We needed something more, something with authority. That night I prayed about it and what came to mind was the flagging I had seen some young men do at the last March for Jesus event in Winnipeg.

The next day I shared that thought with Doug Halstead and asked him if he knew anyone who taught flagging or could visualize this. He seemed strangely silent, then said, "I have done some flagging. As a mater of fact, last night I woke up thinking that if there was one song that I would like to choreograph, it would be 'Let Your Glory Fall' and I proceeded to visualize the choreography."

"But that is the song I was thinking about!" I exclaimed. You see, Doug had not been at the practice the day before, and I had no idea he had done any flagging. BEFORE YOU CALL I WILL ANSWER!

Doug and Esther spent the next two afternoons with the kids learning the songs. Each of the young boys was directed to ask the Lord what name of God he was to declare as he flagged "Let Your Glory Fall." On the handles of the flags that the March for Jesus committee let the boys use they then engraved names of God—omnipotent, ruler, faithful, healer, etc.

As the kids presented the song, we would all pray that God's glory would fall on the people or church we were ministering to. At one small church in the heart of Mexico City, the sermon just happened to be on the connection between death and glory. The point was made that it is only after Jesus died that it is written, "Now is the Son of Man glorified." Seeds must die before flowers burst forth. God can only be glorified in our lives when we die to our rights, our desires, our agendas and learn to forgive. Glory is not selfish adulation but a quiet explosion of beauty in the midst of death. The theme of God's glory came up unexpectedly again after a prayer walk in Mexico City. We had been asked to find something that brings joy to God's heart, something that made Him sad and someone to pray for that we would meet on the street. My eleven-year-old son Luke came back reflecting, "I saw God's glory revealed in a tiny flower growing through a crack in a crumbling wall!"

It seemed fitting that the last time we did the song as a team was when we were asked to offer it as a benediction for the opening of Bethlehem Aboriginal Church, the church that had been given the building in Winnipeg. What was interesting was that, as usual, my husband Doug would play the song live while the kids danced and flagged. On stage at the church a fellow joined in on keyboards partway through, and I marvelled at how well he both knew the song and fit in with the team. Later I found out it was David Ruis, the very man who wrote the song. Go figure!

~

Another scripture that the Lord gave Kathleen as we headed out from Winnipeg was Isaiah 49:8–13…

Chapter 3 ~ Step by Step You'll Lead Me

Thus says the Lord,
  "In a favorable time I have answered You,
  And in a day of salvation I have helped You;
  And I will keep You and give You for a
    covenant of the people,
  To restore the land, to make them inherit the
    desolate heritages;
Saying to those who are bound, 'Go forth,'
  To those in darkness, 'Show yourselves.'
  Along the roads they will feed,
  And their pasture will be on all bare heights.
"They will not hunger or thirst,
  Nor will the scorching heat or sun strike them
    down;
  For He who has compassion on them will lead
    them
  And will guide them to springs of water.
"I will make all My mountains a road,
  And My highways will be raised up.
"Behold, these shall come from afar;
  And lo, these will come from the north and
    from the west..."
Shout for joy, O heavens! And rejoice, O earth!
  Break forth into joyful shouting, O mountains!
  For the Lord has comforted His people
  And will have compassion on His afflicted.

Not everyone thought it was a great idea to travel to Mexico City and Atlanta with a group of kids ages 9–16. They warned us about the heat, the possible food poisoning, how big the city was, how we could get lost and on and on. But God had spoken: we would neither hunger nor thirst nor would the scorching heat strike us down. So in faith we prayed this scripture—that God would restore the desolate places and prepare a highway for His coming. We prayed that, as we were coming from the north and west of Mexico, God would show compassion to the Mexican people.

Remember the prayer picture that God gave Kristy-Anne of a bowl pouring out rainbow-coloured liquid? Well, a pastor of a church in Mexico City spoke to us after one of the services we participated in and said, "I don't know what it is, but ever since the King's Kids have come, there has been light rain and a rainbow in the sky every day. I feel God is telling us that He has not forgotten the Mexican people; He has heard their cries and wants to bless them!"

Chapter 4

Do Not Despise the Day of Small Beginnings

AFTER BEING GREETED in Atlanta by the visual opulence of tents, red soil and people dressed in native dress from around the world, we wound down to go to the registration tent. Now remember, we were to be part of a larger team from Calgary, but each part of the team had to be registered on their own. OOPS—that was one of the things that was not in my trusty red binder, so there was no record of a team coming from Winnipeg. Tired and at the end of a long trip, I did a good job flapping, which didn't really get us anywhere. Then, in my periphery, I thought I recognized someone. Russell! I just about cried.

Scurrying over, we plopped ourselves in front of him and gushed, "What are we going to do? They don't even know we were coming! I promised I would take good care of these kids!"

Again he must have thought, "Oh, here is that crazy woman again!" However, without missing a beat, he hugged us all and assured us there was room in the tent. There were guys' tents and girls' tents...actually, they weren't really "tents"—just poles and coverings. We would stay in the tent with all the other girls from Calgary and the guys would stay in the guys' tent. Relieved, we set up camp, lay down our sleeping bags and soon went to sleep.

At about two in the morning, we were awakened by headlights and the sound of trucks. They stopped outside our tent and we watched, stunned, as more and more people climbed out and came INTO the tent. FIFTY more girls. They must have come from a completely different time zone as they "quietly" settled into the remaining portion of the tent. Then they started jumping up and down because they were so excited. We later learned that they were from Czechoslovakia. Looking at them the next day, my husband commented, "That is the first time I saw so many "checks" bounce!" He and the boys stayed in a tent that was shared with a group from Korea. Early in the morning they would awaken to rustling and whispering as the Korean kids bundled up all their belongings and stacked them neatly at one end of the tent. The Canadian kids rolled over and tried to get some more sleep, waiting for breakfast that came by truck in big green garbage bags: bagels, cream cheese and juice.

Chapter 4 ~ Do Not Despise...Small Beginnings

A few days later, I was having my quiet time in the tent with Marie, feeling a bit overwhelmed with all that was happening and the fact that our little team had not even been registered. "God, we are so insignificant. Why do you have us here?" As we were reading our Bibles, the Lord simultaneously impressed the same scripture on both of our hearts:

> Then he said to me, "This is the word of the Lord to Zerubbabel saying, 'Not by might nor by power, but by My Spirit,' says the Lord of hosts. 'What are you, O great mountain? Before Zerubbabel you will become a plain; and he will bring forth the top stone with shouts of "Grace, grace"' to it!'...Then you will know that the Lord of hosts has sent me to you. Do not despise these small beginnings... (Zechariah 4:6-10a[12])

As I pondered these verses I felt the Lord say to me, "Carolin, don't despise the day of small beginnings. As there was a cloud the size of a man's hand in the sky in Elijah's time that burst open into a torrent, so I will send a downpour of My Spirit!"

I looked up into the blue sky and thanked the Lord for His promise.

A short while later, we made our way to the "Celebration Tent"—but we didn't get there before the rain started to pour. As we looked at each other, we started to giggle, then laugh, jumping up and down in the puddles that were quickly forming. Soaked but happy, we gladly entered into worship.

Section One

Celebrate

As mentioned, when we arrived in Atlanta, we were greeted by a HUGE tent village; 5,000 kids and leaders from the four corners of the earth had come together to worship, all living in tents! To celebrate Jesus! During the day there were "got to know you" activities as we explored cultures and mission strategies around the world. Soccer games, frontier backpacking, playing in the HUGE pool and looking at the displays that each team brought were enjoyed.

Each evening we met in a humongous tent—you know, the kind that golf domes are made out of. Koreans, Fijians Hawaiians, Americans, Germans, Norwegians, Islanders, Spanish, Africans; people from all the continents of the world were in one tent! It was amazing. In the tent there were headphones and translators, and each evening the session was translated into a different language while the others could hear what was going on in their own language through their headsets.

A different continent presented and offered "the glory of their nation" to the King of Kings each evening. The themes varied according to the continent as presentations in dance, sports, drama and song were offered. Young people with fire in their eyes spoke and challenged us all, and a call to the mission field in that continent was given.

Europe presented "Celebrate the only true God!" Germany led the way with a powerful presentation of

Chapter 4 ~ Do Not Despise...Small Beginnings

"We Will Break Dividing Walls," fresh from the victory of the fall of the Berlin wall.

> *Love! God is Love. He showed this to us by sacrificing His only Son's life and by choosing us to be His own. In giving His life, Jesus gave up everything so we could be a part of the eternal covenant of love with His father. Are you willing to give up everything out of your love for Him? As we celebrate His lordship, let's give Him what He deserves and lay down those things in our lives that are fighting for His rightful place; letting no other god come before Him, but covenanting our lives wholly and completely to Him. He is the one true God, no one person or thing compares to Him. Surely this isn't too much to ask. Will you make that radical commitment?*[13]

The Middle East, with their shoes off, celebrated a Holy God:

> *In these days our Father seeks from us that we present ourselves as living sacrifices to Him, holy and acceptable...in other words, that we give Him our best. If we can focus our minds tonight on His awesome greatness, we will be moved to a new place of sincere worship. Moreover, we want to celebrate the fact that such a Holy God can be our God and that He wants our lives to be a fragrant offering to Him. Let us aim to be like Him so that we can grasp just a little bit more of who He is and of His splendor.*[14]

It was a time unlike we had ever experienced as we gathered before the throne of God for hours in worship with every tribe and nation.

Section One

Blessing and honor, glory and power
Be unto the Ancient of Days
From ev'ry nation all of creation
Bow before the Ancient of Days

Ev'ry tongue in heaven and earth
Shall declare Your glory
Ev'ry knee shall bow
At Your throne, in worship

You will be exalted O God
And Your kingdom shall not pass away
O Ancient of Days

Your Kingdom shall reign
Over all the earth
Sing unto the Ancient of Days
For none can compare
To Your matchless worth
Sing unto the Ancient of Days[15]

At the end of the week all 5,000 plus were commissioned to go throughout North and South America on outreach. We were challenged with:

Your battle is not against men and women, but against isolation and segregation. You came not to shed blood, but because His blood was shed, your weapon is your worship and your worship is your weapon. Your clothing is not camouflage, army attire, but a vulnerable open spirit of transparency. Your strategy is not one of dominance, but the posture of a lamb. The greatest need in the Americas and the world is for genuine love and simple acts of kindness. Go in peace, be at peace, and extend the peace of Christ.[16]

As one we responded, "Lord God, we are at Your command. We are willing to go, in the day of Your power. Call forth a new Generation, Lord, from every nation, who will take Your Good News to the ends of the earth. Help us to speak in boldness, yet with words seasoned with Your grace. Stretch out Your hand, Lord, to heal and perform mighty works in and through Your Son, Jesus, our friend and redeemer."[17]

YOU are exalted, Lord, above all else

In Mexico City, we were a part of the larger team from Calgary and Thunder Bay. We did presentations in churches, in parks and in Zocalo square in front of the president's place. The president of Mexico actually came out on the balcony and watched part of the presentation. In each place we shared God's love through worship, dance and drama and handed out scripture passages in Spanish.

We also played with the kids that we met in the parks and on the streets. Some of the younger girls found a stray puppy and were trying to convince us to take it home, but we had to settle with finding a blanket for it and some food. It was quite a sight seeing Doug with five or six of the young girls on the team trailing behind him down the street and through the market while he held the cardboard box with the puppy in it. Soon they were joined by ten, then twenty or more Mexican children who wanted to know what in the world we had in the box and why we were carrying it down the street. When at last we deposited it in a wooded area, wrapped it in the blanket and left food for it, bewildered, these kids looked at us and scratched their heads. Dogs there were mostly guard or stray dogs from what we had seen, and I'm sure they went home with stories about these crazy Canadians...but perhaps God's love for all His creatures was imparted as well.

The highlight for our team was climbing up a mountain just outside Mexico City, the site of an Aztec temple. From the beginning of King's Kids, the declaration of what we understand of the character of God and the evidence of who He is, as seen in His wonderful deeds, have been an emphasis of their public ministry. This declaration was accomplished in our case through worship, dance, drama and intercession. This was different than sharing the Gospel, which we also did in certain places.

God delights in using kids to declare prophetically what He yet purposes to do in a city, nation or area. They are strategic in releasing the power of the Holy Spirit into a nation as well as correcting the distorted picture that many people have of God. We also realize that children and youth have a special God-given capacity to worship. Psalm 8:2 (NIV) says, "From the lips of children and infants you have ordained praise...to silence the foe and the avenger." Often the Lord leads us to minister to Him in places that are satanic strongholds that have brought much grief. This delights Him and shatters the control of the enemy. Just as the children participated in welcoming Jesus into Jerusalem in His triumphant entry the first time, so we believe that God is stirring the hearts of children to worship God in preparation for His second coming."[18]

Thus, as we climbed, we sang and prayed. When we got to the top, we arrived just too late to actually go to the temple, as the gate had been locked twenty minutes before our arrival. Not to be deterred, we sang and worshipped outside the gate for a good hour anyway. "You are exalted, Lord, above all else,"[19] we declared. "We place you in the highest place so the world will know...that you are... *victorious, a mighty warrior, King of Kings, Almighty, most Holy God, faithful, saviour!*"

On the way down we picked up stones of remembrance.

Three days later, we returned to the Winnipeg airport and were greeted with flowers and banners. Jubilant and exhausted, we were embraced as families and friends were reunited. Everyone was accounted for as tears ran down my face.

"We made it!" I exclaimed.

"No one got lost...at least not for very long. Yeah, there was the time when Derek lost his action group in the market...but we won't go there. He found his way home by looking for the "sewer" river that changed colour EVERY day!

"Yeah, they had yellow chickens hanging in the market!"

"Or sick...except for some sniffles here and there and we ALL only drank the bottled water, right?" two of the girls giggled.

"Oh yeah, and did you hear about the earthquake that hit when we landed? Well, we didn't have running water because of it and had to use a bucket to flush!"

"We saw the President of Mexico. He watched us dance! Cool, hey?"

"We had guard dogs on the roof of the place we stayed, and they sold ice cream sort of, in these little cups, with worms on top, at the park."

"They had the CUTEST little kids!"

"You should see them drive there! They had all these green Volkswagen taxis... and the buses—they don't wait for stop lights, they just go! And there are these street kids selling stuff RIGHT IN the traffic...."

We were home.

Section Two

*Lift up your heads, O gates,
And lift them up, O ancient doors,
That the King of glory may come in!*

Ps 24:9

Chapter 5

Start of Daniel Prayer Groups

THROUGHOUT THE FALL of '96, as we reminisced over the summer's outreach, we realized that God had spoken to the team in an unusual way and that there seemed to be a special touch on that particular group of kids. We had a growing sense that we should continue to meet regularly to follow up on the thoughts that the Lord had impressed on our hearts. I phoned Russell and asked him if there was such a thing as a year-round King's Kids team, and he mentioned something about "Daniel Prayer Groups." After some digging, I found some information about this through YWAM Ireland.

Daniel Prayer Groups are a part of King's Kids and consist of groups of kids that meet together to pray for the nations and whatever else God places on their hearts. They started in Ireland at the time of Hurricane Daniel. Some kids and leaders who were meeting together came up with the idea to pray up a prayer storm—like Hurricane Daniel—focusing on the Muslim peoples. I was also intrigued by the story of Daniel in the Bible, a young man who lived such a life of faith that he was able to influence a foreign king to the extent that he acknowledged God. Where were the Daniels in our day who would live a life of no compromise and be able to influence the society around them?

We decided to start a similar group, with the core being the kids from Winnipeg who were part of the Mexico team. The focus would be to pray for the nations and to challenge the kids to live like Daniel did. We would meet once a month, using material we looked up and ideas that the Lord gave us. Creative times of prayer and waiting on the Lord for His strategy were what we would seek to follow. This included praying at the provincial legislative buildings, doing prayer walks in parts of town that He highlighted for us and cleaning up the graffiti in the inner city. We wrote letters of encouragement to government leaders and handed out cookies and apples to people on the street who served the city, such as police officers and street sweepers. At times we focused on praying for the nation by looking in newspapers to find prayer needs. The heart that we sought to instil in the kids was that God is concerned about every facet of our society, be it individual people, cities or nations. Like Samuel, we wanted to take the posture of "Speak, Lord, for your servant is listening" and then, when He spoke, to obey—even if it didn't make a lot of sense.

Chapter 5 ~ Start of Daniel Prayer Groups

These meetings were not like your typical prayer meeting. For instance, we played musical chairs with the prayer needs under the seats. Once, when we were praying for the homeless, we went outside and prayed in cardboard boxes in the snow, with only socks on our feet. It made the point, and it opened our eyes to the reality that many people face in the world. We made tents to pray in when we focused on the people in the Middle East who live in tents. We made a *Sukkoth* or 'booth' built out of branches and leaves during the feast of Tabernacles. This was to remind the Jewish people of how God took care of them in the wilderness and it served as a delightful object lesson in which to pray for Israel. Who doesn't like building a fort and camping outside for a week?

Using prayer tools like a beach ball with the world printed on it, we tossed it from person to person, praying for the nation their hands landed on. A favourite prayer tool was taking a parachute and using it to make a canopy of prayer over a map of the world or a particular nation while we prayed under the parachute.

As I have mentioned, one of the main reasons that we felt led to start these Daniel Prayer groups was to follow up on what the Lord had given us during boot camp and outreach to Atlanta and Mexico. Foundational to the training in King's Kids and YWAM is learning to hear God's voice and respond as He directs. There was a definite sense of God leading us to something, and we felt that this was beyond what had happened during the outreach so far. That was a huge question on our minds. WHAT was it that He was asking of us?

During the summer of '97, a number of us joined Russell in Alberta on a short outreach (you're right, I didn't have to lead this one) to a native reserve where we helped re-roof the church. This was, in our hearts, one further step towards breaking the dividing walls between us and the Aboriginal people. Both their graciousness and the way the kids worked removing insulation in 30-plus degree Celsius temperatures was amazing. At the end, a plaque with the kids' names on it was placed on the church wall. James, the young lad who was with the team in Mexico praying for the walls to be broken down, was right in there with the rest, removing walls literally—the first fruits of his prayers.

Chapter 6

Quebec: Pulling a Team Together

OVER THE NEXT year, as we went back once again to the words that He had given us prior to going to Atlanta and Mexico, we asked the Lord to clarify what was on His heart. One of the newer kids in the DPG group, Karissa, had the impression that there were huge walls between the provinces in Canada, the biggest one being by Quebec. Then she had the impression that the only way these walls would come down was if we proclaimed the name of Jesus at the borders between the provinces. She had not been a part of the team to Mexico, so had not heard this word before.

By now I had a growing sense of the need to take a team to Quebec. It started with the thought, "You shall be my witnesses from Jerusalem to Judea to the ends of the earth." As my mind followed the "rabbit trails" I thought, "Okay, our ministry should start from where we 'started' and then outwards, my Jerusalem being Quebec, since I was born in Montreal."

During a quiet time, the scripture from Ezekiel 36:24–26 leapt out at me:

> *For I will take you from the nations, gather you from all the lands and bring you into your own land. Then I will sprinkle clean water on you, and you will be clean;...I will give you a new heart and put a new spirit within you; and I will remove the heart of stone from your flesh and give you a heart of flesh.*

Very clearly, the thought came that this was speaking about Canada at this time—the provinces being the "nations"—and that if we were to come from across Canada to Canada's Jerusalem, or starting place, God would meet with us and heal our hearts. Besides being where I was born, the first settlers that came to Canada settled in Quebec and actually founded the first mission post there.

This was all before I was aware of the reconciliation movement in Canada and the prayer that Canada's wounds be healed. I had no idea that "nations" could be wounded. In spite of this ignorance, a desire was born to form a team comprised of kids from across Canada: some with roots in Quebec, some able to speak French.

"Oh man, here we go again," I thought. This time Russell hadn't even asked me, yet I had an even stronger sense that I needed to obey God's leading in this. Panic set in at the thought of my actually sug-

Chapter 6 ~ Quebec: Pulling a Team Together

gesting this idea. How does one go about doing this? *"Step by step You'll lead me and I will follow You all of my days."*

So I called Russell. He thought the idea was from God, but suggested that I test it and see if three things would fall into place:

- Gather people to pray.
- Get the leaders for the team in place.
- Seek confirmation from the kids in the DPG group.

Again, the Lord spoke strongly during a quiet time: "My yoke is easy and My burden is light." He promised me that He would lead me and go before me. All I needed to do was to rest and obey His promptings. He assured me that this was HIS team and that HE would pull it together. He impressed on me that any time the task would appear frustrating it would be an indication that I was stepping out from under His yoke. He then told me I was only allowed to work one day a week on this—Wednesday—and leave it for the rest of the week.

If I thought God had gone before us to Mexico, He was about to take us on a whole other adventure now.

Within a week, I was prompted to call Anne's parents in Ontario about being on staff. (After all, Anne was one of the kids who had received the prayer pictures about the walls.) When we had flown though Toronto on the way to Mexico, they had taken the team out for pizza and indicated that at some point they might be interested in being involved on a team.

Section Two

As I now shared with Anne's mom, Brenda, I sensed her excitement as she blurted out, "Chuck and I have had a burden for Quebec for years!" Then she casually stated, "By the way, I teach French, Canadian History and drama." I didn't know any of this before, and yet, what a gift it would be to have someone on the team who could help us understand the historical events that led Canada to be where we were now—someone who was fluent in French and was a drama major, to boot!

The following Sunday, independently of one another, two people from our home church indicated an interest to meet with me to pray for the ministry of King's Kids. I had not yet asked anyone for prayer. When we met with the kids at the next DPG meeting, all of them sensed an excitement that this was, indeed, the right direction. One girl shared a dream that she had recently had in which we were driving across Canada and stopping at the borders to pray for God to heal the divisions between the provinces. Another piped up and said, "I think that the words that God has been giving us are more for Canada and Quebec than Mexico."

"So now," I questioned, "how do I pull together the rest of the team?" Was He calling any of the Daniel Prayer group to go? As I remembered the initial scriptures about God taking us back to our land, I contemplated others who I already knew had roots in Quebec. But whom should I call?

Each morning, after the kids were off to school, I would take out my list of people to call, only to get no

Chapter 6 ~ Quebec: Pulling a Team Together

answer or a busy signal. (This was before e-mail was widely used). I was ready to throw in the towel after three weeks! WHY was no one home? I looked at my calendar...it was Monday...it was Friday..."I've got kids to pick up from school and take to soccer"; "I have a deaconess meeting to go to..."; "...supper and lunches to make..."; Yada-yada-yada... "Why aren't they HOME? This is Your work, God, and I only have a bit of time to do this!"

"My yoke is easy my burden is light." I heard the quiet whisper trying to get past the busyness and confusion.

"What was that? Oh yeah," I sighed, "I don't have to do this on my own...You are leading me. It wasn't Your idea to call these people now, right?"

Again, I gave a big sigh. When would I learn not to take things back into my own hands? Rest enveloped me. I took the controls and gave them back to the Lord. Wednesdays it would be.

As I spent time with the Lord and talked things over with Doug, I became refocused. The original thought had been to gather kids from across Canada, so God had to help me find these kids. As I pondered, thoughts from the past came to me, memories of evenings in worship with loads of young people in a church in Montreal's Lakeshore Evangelical Church. I remembered times at the altar praying with other kids who had long hair and bare feet. I recalled coffeehouses and the passion that was expressed. I recalled Jim Cantelon, the youth leader, challenging us to go to the streets and share our faith with our friends. I wondered where he was now. "Maybe I should get in touch with him to thank him for how he invested in us."

Then I recalled an article from *Christian Week*. In it the story was told of a nine-year-old girl, Tamara O'Reilly, who had gone to Seoul, Korea, to pray at the Global Consultation on World Evangelism. "For the first time in history, children have been invited to participate as praying participants at a conference like this...there is a connection between children's prayer and revival. When God is ready to do something, he causes his people to pray. And Jesus said, 'Don't hinder the children, let them come too!'" said Ester Ilinsky, the head of the Children's Global Prayer Movement.

"Man," I thought, "She would be a good person to have on the team to pray. But HOW can I connect with her? Is she even in Canada?"

In February of 1998, I headed out to Atlantic Canada with Doug to attend some meetings. While there, we took the opportunity to meet and pray with David and Rhonda Peterson, the directors of King's Kids Atlantic Canada. They were SUCH an encouragement and shared how, the previous summer, the Lord led them to take a team of kids to Campbellton, New Brunswick, and pray for Canada. The focus of that team was to bring God's healing to the First Nations people. "The warrior King is rising up in His people to take what belongs to Him and to advance His kingdom in this nation and beyond. These young ones who we are taking out this summer are His young warriors, who will fight with the pure praises of God in their

Chapter 6 ~ Quebec: Pulling a Team Together

mouths, pure lives and repentant praying hearts. Keep that in view," she admonished.

When I returned to Winnipeg, I was greeted by an e-mail that Rhonda had forwarded to my husband at work. "Nationwide call to prayer on the first Friday of every month," it read. The launch of "Canada in Prayer" was both exciting and joyful, but there was an underlying seriousness that made it more of a "Holy Convocation." The agreement to pray was based on 2 Chronicles 7:14 and was a call to the whole body of Christ in Canada to be "Canada in Prayer."[20] I skimmed through the note and screeched to a halt: "Jim Cantelon as host pastor...Tamara O'Reilly, a twelve-year-old intercessor, has a special burden to pray for her generation and asked for the prayers of the older generation."[21]

"God, what is this? I have found the people YOU placed on my heart! Only You could orchestrate this!"

Quickly, I phoned the contact person, Peg Byars, and asked her how I could contact Tamara and Jim. She gave me the information—I guess I didn't sound too crazy. After prayer and a few communications back and forth, Tamara and her mom agreed that yes, this was right.

I had my girl from British Columbia! WHEEE! And it was Tamara, the very one God placed on my heart and who I had NO clue how to connect with. But HE did!

This set a precedent as to how the Lord went ahead and orchestrated all the details of the outreach, from "Puppet Master," the powerful street drama that we were going to do, to the songs for which we would learn choreography: "Rise Up," "Let Your Glory Fall," "Celebrate" and "Peace Be to These Streets." In each case, God brought people with HUGE giftings to train the kids. A core group of kids from the Daniel Prayer Group met weekly for six weeks throughout the spring to learn these pieces, so they would have a head start and therefore make everything easier for the rest of the team to learn once we all came together. The team was also asked to read a book, *The Two Solitudes*, by Hugh Mac Lennon, to give them a better understanding of the cultural struggle between the French and the English.

In mid-July, a week or two before the outreach, I received a phone call out of the blue from a lady by the name of Erica. She had heard a group of King's Kids was coming to Quebec and had taken two weeks of vacation over the time that we would be in town. Her offer was to be available to do anything we needed help with. She mentioned she was associated with St. Stephen's church as the music director. "Okay," I felt, "Let me check this out." I only wanted people on the team that God brought and did not want to be sidetracked by a well-meaning lady on vacation. The only person I could connect with that knew her assured me that she was on the level and a wonderful person! So, "All right Lord, You lead in this one." Did He ever have a surprise in mind! Just when you think you have figured out how God is leading, He does something unexpected.

Chapter 6 ~ Quebec: Pulling a Team Together

As we prayed with our intercessors and with the kids, the goals of the outreach were set:

- To expose kids from outside of Quebec to Quebec culture and to develop God's heart for Quebec.
- To be of service to both French and English churches in the Montreal area through outreach endeavours.
- To promote spiritual reconciliation between French and English Canada through partnering in ministry with local churches and organizations.
- To thank and bless English churches in Quebec for their role in shaping leaders in the rest of Canada.

"However the Lord would lead" would be the key to how we would function. We would come with plans made in pencil, willing to change them if God would lead us in another direction.

Chapter 7

Brownsburg

IN THE EARLY 1970's, God moved in a significant way in revival among the youth of Montreal. It now seemed that many on the King's Kids team that God was pulling together had been inspired in some way by that move of God. Was this an instance of honouring the wells of the past and digging into them?

While I was organizing the outreach, a very clear pattern was emerging. God seemed to be bringing together people who had been involved in an outreach into a small town in Quebec situated close to the Ontario border—Brownsburg. I had not been a part of that outreach, so I did not know the people or the circumstances involved there. But God would put names on my heart, or people would suggest I contact someone, and it would turn out they had somehow been connected to the Brownsburg outreach of 1972.

For example, I heard about a time of prayer in a Montreal Church—St. Stephen's Anglican—focusing on reconciliation and renewal in Quebec. I felt led to contact Robin Guinness, the pastor of St. Stephen's, to ask if, once we arrived in Montreal, he would be able to talk to our team about the needs in Quebec and what we should be praying for. He was more than willing to help and suggested we pull together some other people as well: Pierre Lebel and Rene la Framboise.

A while later, I woke up with the thought, "Call Pierre Lebel." I had heard he was the YWAM director in Montreal, a good place to start, and Robin had just mentioned his name as well. He was home (it was Wednesday). Yes, he would help and we were welcome to communicate with his staff to help us set up venues and accommodations.

"By the way, are you related to the Doug Sadler who was on an outreach team to Lachute in 1972?" he queried.

"Well, my husband's name is Doug, but I don't know of him being in Lachute at that time," I responded. I thought it was interesting that he knew a Doug Sadler as well.

Over supper, I mentioned this to Doug. "You know, I called this guy, Pierre Lebel, and he asked if I knew a Doug Sadler that was involved in an outreach to Lachute in 1972. Do you..."

"Big Pete?" he exclaimed. "Of course I do! He lived in Lachute that summer when we did an outreach in Brownsburg, which was just down the road. I believe he came to the Lord around that time. A group of us "Jesus freaks" took the summer and ran a coffeehouse outreach to the area. We met at a church and there

Chapter 7 ~ Brownsburg

was this pastor who just opened his heart to us...Robin Guinness was his name."

"What?" I exclaimed, "I just spoke with a Robin Guinness last week and he agreed to help us, along with Pierre."

"Yeah, well there was a core team that worked there and gave leadership: Brenda, Anne's mom and Ruth...and we would go there and play music and hand out tracts. We were kind of a raw bunch, but I guess God knew our hearts. We met in what we called 'The Cave' in the basement of an abandoned church."

"Brenda?" I asked, "You mean the Brenda of Chuck and Brenda?"

"Yeah."

"Well, they're already praying about if they should be a part of the team this summer!"

Shortly afterwards, we heard back from Renee, whose dad had come to know Jesus during the summer's outreach in Brownsburg. She, too, felt God calling her to be part of the team, and she lived in Quebec.

What was this connection with Brownsburg?

Before any outreach there is a boot camp, a time when as a team we come together to bond and have times of teaching that are applicable for that particular outreach. Then we ask God what is on His heart for the outreach and learn any performing arts pieces that we might use to minister on the streets or in churches—"fine tune" the team, you might say.

I was asking God to lead us to just the right location for this. In my mind I saw a wooded area away from crowds so we would not be interrupted and would be able to focus. I remembered that we had been at a "chalet" in the woods somewhere close to Montreal on a youth retreat when we were young adults, and as I remembered the place, I thought it would be ideal. It belonged to Lakeshore Church, so I looked up the contact information and shared our heart with them. Listening, they agreed to our using the chalet for our boot camp. When I asked for directions, it turned out to be just outside of Brownsburg.

Two weeks before the outreach, Ruth phoned me. We received their Christmas newsletters and I had phoned her earlier to catch up on family news. In the course of that conversation I told her about the upcoming outreach and ended with, "Pray about if maybe you are supposed to come on the team with your kids." After all, she WAS from Ontario, one of the places from which I did not have any "kids" from—yet. Initially, she didn't seem to have any inclination towards this, but hey, she would pray about it.

Now two weeks before outreach, I still didn't have kids from Ontario. Okay, by now Chuck and Brenda had agreed to go and they were from Ontario. "Maybe that will count," I thought.

Then Ruth called. While in the shower, the Lord had challenged her: "Why can't you and two of the kids go on that outreach? Do you have anything better to do? Call Carolin and ask if they still are interested." So she called, and God's "kids" from Ontario were in place! PLUS she, too, "only" wanted to cook on a team, not lead it, and we did NEED a second cook! AND she had a van—we needed more transportation for kids to get places. To top it off, Ruth was another one of the leaders on the core team for the '72 outreach and her husband who lived in Brownsburg had come to the Lord there. PRAISE GOD FOR SHOWERS!

In the course of our conversation, during which I pontificated with the best of them, I let Ruth know where we were planning to have boot camp. Now SHE was silent. Finally, she told me how, in 1972, she had experienced tremendous restlessness and, after prayer and fasting and through a remarkable chain of events, was led to go to Brownsburg. It had been a life-changing experience for her and one where she was stretched out of her comfort zone. She remembered how she and Doug had painted a scripture on the wall of "The Cave."

> *Then I will sprinkle clean water on you, and you will be clean;...I will give you a new heart and put a new spirit within you; and I will remove the heart of stone...and give you a heart of flesh.*[22]

"I was always prim and proper," Ruth continued, "from a strong Christian family and a staid Brethren church. Suddenly, at age twenty-two, I found myself living and working with a bunch of wild, disorganized, goofy, longhaired, teenaged Pentecostals from Montreal! Most were university or CEGEP students involved with Intervarsity Christian Fellowship who wanted to reach out in evangelism. They had little training themselves and most were young Christians, but they went with the attitude of 'just doing it' the way Jesus did. (CEGEP is a post-secondary college in Quebec.)

"To say that I was stretched out of my comfort zone is an understatement! But God did an amazing thing in my heart that summer; He removed my heart of stone and gave me a heart of flesh. That's why I always remembered that verse that we painted on the wall…it reflects what happened to me in that place. God expanded my vision and my heart so I could embrace those different from me," she told me.

Full circle—the very scripture that God had prompted me with to start this venture. We both wept. I was so looking forward to getting to know this lady and her kids beyond the Christmas newsletters. Our God is an awesome God!

Of the team of twenty-four, nine members had either been involved in the outreach in '72 or were children of those affected by that outreach. In addition, there were three people connected to the earlier outreach who were instrumental in helping with contacts for this present one. Up until boot camp we still did not know why God had so carefully orchestrated this.

"A prayer walk—sending forth life instead of death"

Early one morning during boot camp, as a team we all felt that we really needed to ask the Lord why He had led us to this place in particular. So we had a time of worship and asked Him. "God, open our eyes to see Your agenda here. We don't see it, but we want to do Your will and not miss what You have for us."

Chapter 7 ~ Brownsburg

We got out the map and realized that Brownsburg was located close to the junction of the Ottawa and St. Lawrence Rivers, where English Canada meets French Canada. It was also in Quebec, just across the Ontario border. Ruth then started to share what her husband, Tuck, had told her about the history of Brownsburg. He said that Brownsburg was a picture in miniature of Quebec and its conflicts—with the "French hill" and the "English valley." The two people groups were divided physically and emotionally, as evidenced by the degree of negative sentiment in their town. This was most noticeable in the local high school. She also shared that there was a factory in Brownsburg that had manufactured weapons for the Second World War, and these explosives had been tested in a large field in the vicinity.

As a group we felt led to do a prayer walk in Brownsburg to pray for healing in the community and also to pray at the factory that was located right on the banks of the river. We divided into four groups and from the center of town we spread out, agreeing to meet back in a park right opposite to where "The Cave" had been. As we walked and prayed, we asked the Lord that somehow this area of Canada would become a centre from which His love and life would flow out to the rest of Canada and to the world instead of being a center of conflict and destruction. We had a time of prayer at the factory, looking down from the bridge over the river and declaring, "Let this be a place from which Life flows instead of death." And yes, when we all got together again in the centre of town we sang, danced and flagged, "Let your glory fall, let it go from here to the nations."

In Ruth's words, "To go back to Brownsburg was a very powerful experience for me. To pray outside the core team house and with Brenda and Doug on the church steps were unbelievably emotional moments. I am so thankful to God for once again allowing me the privilege of seeing His hand at work in us in that special town." The kids were amazed to see God work out these details, and we wondered what possible fruit would come out of our simple prayers.

The following November, we learned that the new "March for Jesus" CD was being recorded in Morin Heights, which is located just north of Brownsburg in a studio upstream from the place by the river where we had prayed. The title of the CD was "Lord of Life!" by Russ Rosen's band, "Upstream." This was the first March for Jesus recording that was bilingual—French and English—a uniquely Canadian CD that God used to minister this unity in Canada and worldwide.

A copy of the CD went to Rwanda, where Canadians were held in high regard because of the work of Canadian peacekeepers during the genocide of the 1990's. A group of Rwandan pastors extended an invitation to Upstream to bring a team of Canadians to work with them, fostering reconciliation and doing outreach in Rwanda. Russ's band led the team and Doug was able to go along. That started a HUGE connection for him that is still being walked out. But that is a whole other story.

Chapter 8

Why Montreal?

"ONE OF THE great symbols of Montreal is its cross. This cross was erected in 1924 and recalls the time January 6, 1643 when Sieur de Maisonneuve, the founder of Montreal, ordered a wood cross be planted on Mount Royal. There had been a flood in 1642 that was threatening the settlement of Ville Marie, Montreal's original name. The leaders prayed that if the flood receded they would put up a cross on the Mountain. The present cross on the mountain is obviously not the same cross, but it is a reminder of God's saving grace."[23]

Ville Marie was founded May 17, 1642. After stepping out of a boat and putting his feet in the soil, Maisonneuve dropped to his knees to adore God. They all sang psalms and hymns to the Lord. The purpose of the colony was to "bring about the glory of God"[24] and salvation to the people. These are Canada's spiritual foundations, the first mission being in Quebec, where people prompted by the Holy Spirit came to bring a witness of His love to this nation.

Psalm 24 became a focal point as the King's Kids team prayed for the outreach:

> ¹ *The earth is the Lord's, and all it contains,*
> *The world, and those who dwell in it.*
> ² *For He has founded it upon the seas*
> *And established it upon the rivers.*
> ³ *Who may ascend into the hill of the Lord?*
> *And who may stand in His holy place?*
> ⁴ *He who has clean hands and a pure heart,*
> *Who has not lifted up his soul to falsehood*
> *And has not sworn deceitfully.*
> ⁵ *He shall receive a blessing from the Lord*
> *And righteousness from the God of his salvation.*
> ⁶ *This is the generation of those who seek Him,*
> *Who seek Your face—even Jacob. Selah.*
> ⁷ *Lift up your heads, O gates,*
> *And be lifted up, O ancient doors,*
> *That the King of glory may come in!*
> ⁸ *Who is the King of glory?*
> *The Lord strong and mighty,*
> *The Lord mighty in battle.*
> ⁹ *Lift up your heads, O gates,*
> *And lift them up, O ancient doors,*
> *That the King of glory may come in!*

On July 1st, 1998, I was asked to share on "It's a New Day," a national Christian television program, the thoughts behind the journey we were about to embark on. How was God going to bring down the walls of division in our nation—remove the stones, so to speak—and lay a "highway of holiness" for His glory?

Chapter 8 ~ Why Montreal?

"Montreal was founded upon the rivers at the eastern gateway to Canada. Did God lead people to found it and establish a mission, name it Ville Marie and one of the Islands 'Isle de Jesus' and then walk away, letting time and chance run its course? No," I stated. "God cares very much about Canada and Quebec and Montreal. The roots of Canada are very spiritual, but we have fallen far from God." But we are reminded that:

> *If my people, who are called by my name, will humble themselves and pray and seek my face and turn from their wicked ways, then will I hear from heaven and will forgive their sin and will heal their land.*[25]

"God wants to heal and cleanse our hearts and land literally," I declared.

"So," I continued, "twenty-seven of us from across Canada, representing seven provinces, will head off to the first mission post in Canada, Canada's Jerusalem, to humble ourselves and pray that God would heal our land. We are not even talking about national unity. We need to go before that and seek God's forgiveness for how we have wounded each other and Him.

"Who may ascend the hill of the Lord? He who has clean hands and a pure heart. We are seeing more and more that it is a pure righteous life and passionate love for Jesus that is the greatest weapon against the enemy. We, as the emerging generation, want to be the generation of those who seek the Lord, as it says in Psalm 24. WHY? So the King of glory may come in.

Lord, only You can heal the deep hurts across Canada. Let Your glory fall on this place, as even Maisoneuve, the founder of Montreal, prayed...and let it go forth to the nations. We need to bow before a holy God, we need to come with individual and corporate repentance, one heart at a time, before God, in unity first with God and then with each other."[26]

En Route

On July 29th, as we set out for Montreal, each member of the team was instructed to pray as they crossed the borders of the provinces, whether driving or flying, in response to Karissa's dream about us driving across Canada and praying at the borders. We set out with a vanload of kids. When we reached the Manitoba/Ontario border, we stopped to pray the Lord's Prayer and shouted the name of "Jesus" again, referring back to the prayer pictures given before the Mexico trip. The miles flew by as we picnicked, some of us eating cans of cold "Zoodles," sang, played games and enjoyed the gorgeous scenery of the Great Lakes. We stopped at the occasional rapids along the way, getting soaked of course, or jumped down HUGE sand hills we found in a construction lot. It was a blast!

On our way through Ontario, we had to stop and pick up Karissa, as she had gone ahead to visit her grandparents. As we pulled into the driveway, their phone rang and Karissa beckoned to me from the front door to come and answer it. It was her dad, phoning from Winnipeg, and he wanted to speak with

Chapter 8 ~ Why Montreal?

me. He had no way of knowing when I was going to arrive there, for I had not specified any time other than just sometime in the afternoon, so it was amazing that we connected. He encouraged me and recalled how, when a few people had met together to pray the evening before for the outreach, they had received a caution from the Lord. He said that the phrase, "beware of a thorn in the foot" was impressed on them. I had no idea what this was all about, but kept it tucked away in the back of my mind.

When we arrived at boot camp, people who I had only met on the phone started arriving. By the end of the evening, everyone was at the chalet. I started crying. Amazing, totally amazing! It had worked! They were ACTUALLY all there. What a time we had, learning the presentation pieces in a field covered knee high with wild flowers and ragweed. *ACHOO!!* We were "well furnished" with outhouses and one cold water pump. If we made it through this, we would have bonded well. Out of the corner of my eye, I noticed someone in a long white dress carrying a basket, getting out of a car. I was distracted at that point and didn't see where she went, but thought, "Whatever, I'll get to that later."

Going to "the loo" a short time later, I noticed a transformation. In each outhouse was a spray bottle of perfume and some hand wipes. There were even pictures on the doors! Erica had struck! Why did I ever doubt God's leading? She set the tone as she quietly ministered to the team and just seemed to be wherever she was needed. Then, in one hour, she taught us to sing in four part harmony and in five different languages: "We are walking in the light of God!" Amazing!

At last, the team was ready, and off we left for our first meeting at St. Stephen's church. On the way, we saw light piercing through the clouds over the city of Montreal as different parts of the city were bathed in the golden glow of early morning. The kids all noticed this, for repeatedly during our prayer times they had seen or received words about Light piercing the darkness over Quebec. When we drove over the bridge onto "l'isle Jesu," Graham Kendrick called out, "He is Lord of the Islands," on the tape we were playing and started singing, "The Lord is come. Hosanna, Hosanna, the Lord has come in glory and power...give praise to His name!"[27]

We cheered and could not believe our ears. The "chance" of the tape being in just that spot at just that time brought all of us into a deep time of wonder as we asked God to reveal His presence and do just as the tape had declared. When we arrived at the church, we KNEW that God was with us. On the banner at the front of the church it was written, "Arise; shine for Your light has come."

Our Pace or God's Pace?

At the end of the service we had a delightful lunch and met a number of Montreal's Christian leaders, who shared with us and gave us a better understanding of the needs in Quebec. We learned that it was a province where there was a lot of darkness. There was a high suicide rate, alcoholism, cancer was prevalent, and among the people there was a deep sense of abandonment. The percentage of Christians in Quebec was also minimal. At that time there was a lot in the news about the Bloc Quebecois and the referendum, with many in Quebec seeking to separate from the rest of Canada. The province was also still reeling from a terrific ice storm that had paralyzed it that previous winter. One pastor shared that he longed for the day when the Holy Spirit would fill the nets to overflowing with those responding to the Gospel of grace.

The leaders then gathered around the team and commissioned us, sending us out with their blessing. Off we went, doing presentations—at the mouth of the subway system, in the centre of the business section of town, at inner-city missions, in French and English churches, in a camp for kids—singing, "Peace, Love, Joy be to these streets," and calling out for "JESUS" to break the bondages that people were in.

With such a busy schedule, a number of us had a hard time sleeping the first five days. Up until then, we had been grateful for the accommodations, but there had been no showers, just a wash in shifts under the ice cold water pump at boot camp. We now also had to sleep on the floor. I was exhausted and didn't have the emotional energy to lead the team anymore. As I sat in a corner crying quietly, I thought I should reread the scripture from Joshua that the Lord had previously given me concerning this outreach.

As I read, I was reminded to be strong and courageous and that the Lord would be with us, leading us.

I read a few verses further and came across: *"The Lord your God gives you rest and will give you this Land."*[28] I strongly sensed God speaking to me with concern: "My Yoke is easy, My burden is light. Remember, Carolin, when you are out from under MY yoke you will be tired. I want you to teach the team about entering into My rest."

Through amazing circumstances that only God could have orchestrated, when we came back from our ministry time later that day we were told that we had another place to stay that evening, one with showers and mattresses and large kitchen facilities. That night I slept on a beautiful mattress on the floor. It had been donated to the Salvation Army during the ice storm and had not found a home yet. While the adults appreciated the $3000 mattresses (you know, the kind with the pillow tops), the kids were overjoyed at the boxes of Joe Louis and Twinkies that greeted them. God cares about the big and the small, and He delighted in watching the kids stuffing their faces with cake. It may have seemed like a small thing in the scope of the whole outreach, but it communicated loudly to all of us that God cared. He was concerned about all of life and had not called us to burn ourselves out but to rest in Him. This was His project, after all.

A few days later, we noticed that there were a few kids who had minor injuries to their feet or legs: bruising and twisted or swollen ankles. We prayed for them and went on. Then more injuries occurred and Kitty got a sliver in her foot. Within a day, this sliver turned into an infection with angry red streaks starting up her leg. We took her into the emergency room at the Children's Hospital, where she was immediately told to rest and was given antibiotics as she had the beginnings of blood poisoning. The word that was given us on our way to Quebec flooded back. "Beware of a thorn in the foot!"

By now, we had "clued in" that this was an attack of the enemy and we all sensed an urgency to pray. We gathered around those with injuries, now measuring one third of the team, and proclaimed the scripture, "How beautiful on the mountains are the feet of those who bring good news, who proclaim peace."[29] So, in the name of Jesus, we anointed the injured with oil and declared that these were precious feet and that the enemy had no right to touch them. As the kids laid their hands on those who were hurt, one young boy from Alberta, Jordan, started pulling the tensor bandage off his knee. With tears running down his face, he cried, "The swelling's gone down. I can run!" and proceeded to run around the room. Brenda, who had markedly swollen ankles, found that her swelling went down as well. Most of the other injured were well within a day or so, and no further injuries occurred during the outreach.

What impact did that have? Kitty was awed that God cared enough about her and the team to warn us beforehand. Sharing at a service the next day, my son Shawn said, "I believe that God allowed the injuries on our team as a physical manifestation of the woundedness of Canada. Just as God is able to heal and did heal us, so He will heal Canada." That happened to take place at Lakeshore Church, which a number of the team had attended in the early '70's and where Jim Cantelon had discipled us. As the team presented on stage, one of the women in the congregation looked on with a huge smile. After the presentation, she came forward with tears in her eyes. During the early '70's, she had been doing door-to-door witnessing and had led a lady named Donna Peterson to Christ. One of our team members, Holly Peterson, was Donna's granddaughter. To see the third generation affected by this act of witnessing was overpowering.

The same morning, another whole family had come to see Chuck, whom they had taken into their home off the streets in the early '70's. At that time he had been deeply involved in the drug culture. And now, here he was with Doug (who no longer had waist length hair), singing at the top of their lungs, "Let Your Glory Fall." At the end of the service, the kids were asked to pray for any who had needs, and full of faith, they prayed for the sick, amazed at God's answers to prayer. Yes, truly God can heal and will heal—hearts as well as bodies. The whole team saw God's power at work, and those who were healed will never forget.

Chapter 9

Light Be!

As I mentioned in the last chapter, during our prayer times with the kids, some of them received prayer pictures of "light." In their pictures, light seeped in and started taking over the darkness or light broke through and, wherever it touched the ground, domes of light would appear. Just as at the beginning, in Genesis, the earth was formless and void and darkness covered the earth and God called out "Light Be" and there was light, we were starting to sense that God was asking us to declare "Light Be" over Quebec.

A song that dovetailed with these impressions was "Children of Light,"[30] by Andy Park, as well as the scripture in 1 John 1:5–7, "...God is Light, and in Him there is no darkness at all... if we walk in the Light as He Himself is in the Light, we have fellowship with one another." Another scripture that came to light (no pun intended): "Let your light so shine before men...and glorify your Father who is in heaven."[31] This we asked God to help us walk out: that we would no longer hide our light under the bushel but that we would let it shine. We prayed that God would remove fear and by doing so that it would break the darkness off our peers and also over Quebec. One of the girls really struggled with fear, and we were able to minister to her one evening. The result was visible—she was radiant—and for a long while afterwards, everything she signed ended with "I am a child of light." Her enthusiasm became a catalyst for others in the months ahead.

As we prepared our hearts to minister in the Montreal area, the Lord led us to passages in Joshua chapters 1–3. He encouraged us to be strong and courageous, to go wherever He led us, even if it meant a change of our plans. He called us to set ourselves apart and to consecrate ourselves. This theme of consecration was especially strong one afternoon before we were going to climb up Mount Royal, so we had a time of prayer and washed each other's feet as a sign humility, serving one another and consecrating ourselves anew to the Lord. Following that, the leaders from Montreal that were present prayed with the team leaders over the kids...clean hands and a pure heart.

As we headed out, we had a strong sense that God was going before us. Flashbacks to my childhood, when I had actually lived on Mt. Royal and where my dad was a landscaper, flooded my mind as I looked at the wooded beauty and nicely appointed gardens. When we got to the top of the mountain, we stood around the cross that was erected there and prayed facing outwards, 360 degrees over all of Montreal, singing, "Shout to the north and the south, sing to the east and the west: Jesus we declare you as saviour of all, only You are Lord of heaven and earth!"[32] As we sang, the quietest team member shouted out, "DID you see that? An angel came down and went right down into the city in front of where I was praying!" Excited, we started declaring "Yes, Lord, send your angels into Quebec. LIGHT BE in the darkness!"

We then felt that God was leading two of the boys—both named Luke, which means "Bringer of light"—to pray for the French and English peoples. One Luke from London, Ontario, had a totally British background. The other was my son Luke, who has some French roots. As they stood at the top of Mount Royal, they asked God to forgive any bitterness and pride between them as people groups, and then as a prophetic act that God would bring the two peoples together, they hugged one another—quickly. After all, they were thirteen-year-old boys.

Last of all, we picked up stones to represent the different provinces and built an altar at the foot of the cross as a reminder of what we had done. Renee, the girl from Quebec whose dad had been saved in Brownsburg in 1972, sang a song she had thought of, "Down at Your feet, O Lord, is the most high place, in Your presence, Lord, we seek Your face..."[33]

As we went down the mountain, we stopped at the outlook over the city and saw the bridges, which go out at 360 degrees all around the island. So, in groups of three, we stood at the different lookout points facing these bridges and petitioned that Canada would be used by God to bring healing to the nations.

The Rainbow and L'Église Des Patriotes

A day or so later, Renee mentioned to us that there was a particular church in the St. Eustache area, "L'Église des Patriotes" (meaning "the church of the patriots"), where she felt a strong leading for us to go and pray. Changing our original plans, we headed to St. Eustache and were glad we did. We learned that during a confrontation between the French and English on December 14, 1837, this church had been bombed with cannons and forty-five French Patriots identified as killed.[34] Brenda was able to tell us more of the church's history and how the French farms had been burned at the beginning of the winter and the patriots had fled, seeking refuge in this very church. We could see the dents in the wall where the cannonballs had hit and felt we were to pray over these visible marks for healing and forgiveness. We sensed God's presence so clearly!

The Ezekiel 36:24–26 scripture came back to mind:

> *For I will take you from the nations, gather you from all the lands and bring you into your own land. Then I will sprinkle clean water on you, and you will be clean;...I will give you a new heart and put a new spirit within you; and I will remove the heart of stone from your flesh and give you a heart of flesh.*

Chapter 9 ~ Light Be!

As we were singing and praying, a light rain started to fall and a rainbow appeared in the sky. It was the only time during the whole outreach that it rained while we were outside ministering.

Right after we prayed over the marks left by the cannonballs, the church custodian, who was wondering what in the world we were doing, invited us to come into the church. He was so touched when we asked permission to sing "Let Your Glory Fall" as a blessing. It was just magnificent—the acoustics were incredible and we knew we had brought joy to God's heart. Later, someone told us that it was a miracle that we would have been allowed to sing there in English, as the church was located in an area of town that was not usually open to English. As a team, we knew God had gone before us and perhaps had used us to start the healing of some of the wounds of the people in this area of Montreal.

From L'Église des Patriotes we went to the largest Catholic Church in Quebec, St. Joseph's Oratory. Again we prayed for God's glory to come, and one of the girls saw a clear prayer picture of the place being filled with people—French and English—worshipping God together. Doug mentioned that this had happened before, in the '70's during the revival movement in Montreal at a mass rally for Christ. It was actually that very place, he said, where he first saw God move in power. So we prayed that once again this church would be filled to overflowing; that it would be a place where English and French, Protestant and Catholic could come together in unity; and that, like all the candles that were lit throughout the church, God's Light would come into Quebec and dispel the darkness.

That was also the day that one van whose driver was confident that they knew the way somehow took another route and, after much wandering through the maze of the Montreal highway system, ended up back at the Salvation Army Center. When the rest of the team returned to the Center, we found our "lost" team members, higher than a kite and singing and bouncing off the walls. They did not have a key to the place, so they couldn't get in, and their van had carried the "Twinkies" and other deserts for the whole team. Since they didn't know how long the rest of us would be, guess what they had for supper? It didn't help that the most active kids happened to be in THAT van!

On another occasion, we did a prayer walk in a French neighbourhood, praying that many of the people who lived there would come to know Jesus. This was in co-operation with a French Pastor who was reaching out in that area of town. As we walked, a number of the kids noticed a strip mall where one of the stores was a "strip joint." They were disturbed by this and decided to ask God what He wanted to do about it. They felt that God wanted them to pray in the opposite spirit—that this "yucky place" would close down and that it would become a church instead. We really didn't think we would ever hear about this again, but a year or two later, Erica, who had been one of the people praying there who also lived in Montreal, happened to drive by the neighbourhood. Guess what

Chapter 9 ~ Light Be!

she saw? A brand new storefront church on the very spot where the strip joint had been! As Kristy-Anne says, "Does God speak to kids? UH, DUH, YOU BET!"

During the outreach, Chuck kept on saying, "This is HUGE." And to humour him, I agreed, but I really had no idea of the significance of what we were doing. We were just a group of people out doing what we felt the Lord was telling us to do.

The kids each went home with a blue candle to remind them to continue to pray for Quebec and to "keep the candle burning" of the love that God had lit in their hearts. (The Quebec flag, inaugurated in 1948, is blue and white and has four fleurs-de-lis and a cross. Interestingly, Israel was founded that same year and also has a blue and white flag.) They were also given a "breastplate" with the names of the provinces and the provincial flowers on it. On the back of the breastplate was written this phrase: "Let the walls come down, let us seek unity, kneel in true repentance, and let the glory fall."

After we arrived home from the outreach, I received an e-mail from Renee. She wrote, "God seems to be working really fast in accord with us." That week there had been a debate and decision in the Supreme Court concerning the referendum law in Quebec. "Do you fully realize what the Supreme Court ruling means?" she asked. "Even after a positive referendum, this province could not separate without the agreement of the rest of Canada. Also, both sides were not further wounded by the decision. Isn't it something? Or should I say isn't HE someone!"

Section Two

A few months later, Peg Byars invited me to come to Montreal as a follow up to the outreach and to connect with the people from "Canada in Prayer." During the outreach, she had diligently sent out the team's prayer requests through the Canada in Prayer network. I was so looking forward to meeting with her and sharing at length. The meetings were held at a church in the heart of Montreal, right across the street from St. Stephen's Church. At one point, the two of us went across the street to St. Stephen's to meet Erica in the parish hall, the same room where, that summer, we had met with the kids and had been commissioned by the pastor and leaders from Montreal. As we reflected on the previous summer, Erica suddenly dug into her purse, turned to me and said, "Carolin, you have to listen to this tape!"

RISE UP together everybody
Stand up together God's people
For it's your hour, and by His power
This Land will see the coming of the Spirit of God.

We have the truth for this Nation,
God's way the way of salvation,
We'll do our part, the fire will start,
This Land will see the coming of the Spirit of God.

Every Valley shall be lifted up
And every High place brought down
The crooked ways shall be straightened out
To make a highway for our God and King

Rise up in the power of His word
Rise up, in the name of the Lord.
Rise up, for in unity we stand
Rise up, take His love to all lands
Rise up!
Rise up!
Rise Up![35]

Section Three

Therefore say, "Thus says the Lord God, 'I will gather you from the peoples and assemble you out of the countries among which you have been scattered, and I will give you the land of Israel.'"...And I will give them one heart, and put a new spirit within them. And I will take the heart of stone out of their flesh and give them a heart of flesh, that they may walk in My statutes and keep My ordinances and do them. Then they will be My people, and I shall be their God.

Ezekiel 11:17–20

Chapter 10

Apples and Direction

BACK HOME, I quickly got caught up in the usual: laundry, driving kids to judo, dance, music lessons, part-time work and so on. So it was a few weeks later when I was cleaning out my bottomless purse before I discovered the tape that Erica had given me. OOPS! "I really should listen to it," I mused. When I did, it jolted me awake! To put what I heard in context, let me share some background.

> *There is a place where God has chosen throughout centuries to birth His journeys: in the hearts of men whose sole desire was to seek first the kingdom of God. In 1991, Pastor Bob Birch, an 82-year old man of devoted prayer, tested faith, deep humility felt to gather together a team of young men who would covenant to give themselves constantly to prayer, to hear what the Spirit was*

saying to the church. "To watch and pray," Pastor Bob would say, "is the call of every Christian."

This new team was soon christened "Watchmen for the Nations", drawing its name from Isaiah 62:6–7. "I have posted watchmen on your walls, O Jerusalem; they will never be silent day or night. You who call on the LORD, give yourselves no rest, and give Him no rest till He establishes Jerusalem and makes her the praise of the earth."

The Watchmen team was guided by this simple principle: earnestly seek the face of the Lord for what is on His heart and only do what He says. They even made a covenant with one another not to initiate any programs or plans unless they had a clear word from the Lord that was discerned by the group and confirmed. Only then would they move.

For years, they watched and waited. Praying and asking the Lord to reveal His heart for Canada.

Among those who had joined Pastor Bob and the Watchmen team was a young Egyptian named David Demian. David had come to Canada from Egypt in 1988, and, after some time, had become a traveling companion for Pastor Bob.

In 1994, David had an encounter with a prophet that would change both his life and the direction of Watchmen. This prophet spoke to him about a conference, a gathering that needed to take place the next year.

After God had moved so powerfully at the Whistler and Victoria Gatherings, the Watchmen team expected the church to move quickly into a journey of healing the deep wounds and divisions in the nation. But despite sincere attempts at reconciliation between people groups, breakthrough

> remained elusive. The team was driven to cry out to God to reveal what was the root issue holding back God's favor from the nation. Why were God's prophetic promises for Canada unfulfilled? And why were warnings of judgment increasing?[36]

As I listened to Erica's tape, my heart was gripped with a great sense of unworthiness. I realized that God had called us to be a part of something "HUGE." We had unknowingly been involved in praying for something that God had also put on the hearts of many others in Canada. We were not alone!

On the tape, David Demian passionately shared how, in September 1997, the Lord revealed to him that it was a root of anti-Semitism, which had come to Canada via Europe, that was at the heart of the nation's divisions. After some research, it came to light that this was evidenced most clearly by Canada refusing entrance to over 900 German Jews aboard the St. Louis ship who were fleeing persecution by the Nazi regime before the onset of the Second World War.

> They had sought refuge and were denied entrance in Cuba and the USA. Canada was their last hope. Mackenzie King, who was Canada's Prime Minister at that time, was ultimately responsible for denying sanctuary in Canada during WWII to these people sealing the death warrant for two thirds of the people aboard the St. Louis ship. The response to their plight was "None is too many!" as written in a book by that title by two Canadian professors.[37] Their book detailed even more graphic

> *instances of Canada's anti-Semitic immigration policies which prevented 1,000 orphaned children from finding refuge. The Lord tested the hearts of the government and the people at that time, and we fell short."*[38]

These words disturbed me deeply. The Lord then strongly prompted me to go back to what He had given the Daniel Prayer Group kids the previous fall, in October 1997.

At that time, along with the DPG, we had been seeking the Lord as to what He would have us do in the summer of 1999. The Pan Am games were going to be in Winnipeg that summer and we thought that maybe we should be involved in outreach during these games. (YWAM had set a precedence of doing outreaches at international sporting events.) A huge sporting event was planned for July right in Winnipeg. "It's a no-brainer," I figured.

We followed the steps of waiting on the Lord, fully expecting strategies for an outreach to these games. One of the kids, Holly, received a very clear prayer picture. It was of an apple that fell on Canadian soil, a nice shiny red apple. After a little while it was picked up and passed around, but no one wanted it. It was then tossed back to the ground, but this time it had a swastika engraved on the side. Luke also had a word: "Be not deceived and therefore be ineffective."

We journalled these thoughts, but at that time they really did not make any sense.

Now, a year later, I was rereading the story of the apple. On the first read, something resonated in my

Chapter 10 ~ Apples and Direction

spirit but I still didn't get it. I asked Doug, "Is there any significance about an 'apple' in scripture?" He replied, "Well, if I recall rightly, in Zechariah 2:8 God refers to the Jewish people as the 'Apple of His eye.'"

I looked it up and he was right: *"For he who touches you [Israel], touches the apple of His eye."*

But what did that mean in this context?

All of a sudden, it became clear. The apple represented the Jewish people on the St. Louis! They, too, had been passed around, not wanted and branded by the swastika under the Nazi regime. But how did this effect what we were supposed to do in the summer of 1999?

On April 2nd, the Daniel Prayer Group gathered together to share these thoughts and to seek the Lord. He impressed a number of scriptures on our hearts. One of the boys read from Daniel 9 and suggested that we were to seek the Lord in sackcloth and ashes and that God was going to release travail and supplication.[39] "Holiness and tears are very important, I think," expressed one of the young girls. Johnathan read from Zechariah 3:3–9 (NIV):

> *Now Joshua was dressed in filthy clothes as he stood before the angel. The angel said to those who were standing before him, "Take off his filthy clothes."*
>
> *Then he said to Joshua, "See, I have taken away your sin, and I will put rich garments on you."*

> *Then I said, "Put a clean turban on his head." So they put a clean turban on his head and clothed him, while the angel of the Lord stood by...*
>
> *"This is what the Lord Almighty says: 'If you will walk in my ways and keep my requirements... I will remove the sin of this land in a single day.'"*

After reading this, he reflected, "I think that if we pray really hard—so much that we actually cry because we are really sorry—then God will take away the dirty clothes, which mean the sin, and give us a new start. In ONE day it says! But only if we promise to walk in holiness."

Eleven days later,

> *On April 13, 1999 (Holocaust Memorial Day), eighty-eight intercessors from across Canada, boarded a train in Vancouver bound for Winnipeg. They felt the Lord had asked them to "fill the land with tears." On this Train of Tears, the intercessors fasted, wept and prayed for three days, asking God to have mercy upon Canada. In His wisdom, God used the train, a powerful symbol of Canadian unity, to begin to redeem the memory of the millions transported on trains to suffering and death in Hitler's concentration camps.*[40]

The last stop for the Train of Tears was in Winnipeg, and we were on hand to greet them. Instead of being sent to a death camp, they were embraced with flowers and grapes and cheeses.

It soon became clear that God was leading many Christians in Canada to have a "Gathering" in Winnipeg, the heart of Canada, during the summer of 1999.

Chapter 10 ~ Apples and Direction

It was to be under the banner of Watchmen for the Nations and the vision that God had given David Demian. It was a prayer gathering, the sole purpose of which was to pray for God's glory to fill our land and to start to remove any hindrances or "stones of offence" that stood in the way. This would be a first step—repenting for this anti-Semitic act—and was to be the beginning of a journey of repentance in Canada.

Blow a trumpet in Zion
Consecrate a fast, proclaim a solemn assembly
Gather the people, sanctify the congregation,
Assemble the elders
Gather the children and nursing infants[41]

Once we realized that God was calling us to be a part of this, we contacted a number of the people who had been on the mission trip to Quebec the previous summer. I explained what I had learned, and in response, about half of the team eagerly made their way to Winnipeg. On July 1st, a year to the day after I had shared on the television program about God calling us to pray for His glory to fill our nation and to remove the stones of offence, over 2300 people gathered in Winnipeg to seek the Lord "with a broken and contrite heart."[42]

They were joined by thousands more on July 1st, when David Mainse of Crossroads Communications broadcast the repentance live for 4 hours by satellite throughout the nation.[43]

Section Three

Deep crying filled the meeting hall such as we had never before witnessed. A two-year-old on his father's shoulders echoed the remorse. "I am SO sad!" he said, with tears running down his cheeks.

At the end of our time together, we sensed that God had heard our prayers. Prior to the Gathering, we had been asked to bring stones from significant places or from where God had met us in the past. With these stones we all laid down an altar of remembrance to signify the day that a remnant of Christians in Canada asked God to forgive her for her Anti-Semitism. Renee brought a stone from St. Eustache and Kitty and I brought stones from Mexico, the site of the Aztec temple, where we declared *that God was exalted above all else.* (A week later, we learned that the flame for the Pan Am games taking place in Winnipeg the following week was taken from that very Aztec temple in Mexico where we had worshipped the Lord.)

After the altar was laid, a HUGE double rainbow filled the sky. "Never again" will people in Canada be silent in regards to its stand towards Israel.

> *I set MY BOW in the cloud, and it shall be for a sign of a covenant between Me and the earth....and I will remember My covenant, which is between Me and you and every living creature of all flesh; and NEVER AGAIN shall the water become a flood to destroy all flesh.*[44]

This re-iterated a statement by the then Prime Minister of Canada, Jean Chrétien, who had gone to visit the Nazi death camps in February, a few months earlier. It was the first time that a Canadian Prime Minister visited the death camps. As he stood there beside the head of the Canadian Jewish congress, he said to the world: "Never again."

Chapter 11

Next Steps

A FEW MONTHS later, I was invited to attend a Watchman for the Nations leadership meeting in Ottawa. While there, David casually asked, "When are you taking a team to Israel?"

I sputtered, "I don't know," and wondered where that had come from. I really didn't want to form an outreach team just because it looked like a good idea—not unless God totally made it clear that this was His plan. Israel?

However, the thought was a seed in my spirit, and over the next few months, Israel and things concerning Israel kept crossing my path. I heard of a group of Aboriginal people, led by Linda Prince, who had taken native drums that had the names of the twelve tribes of Israel written on them to Israel. Roger Armbruster, who heads up "Canada Awakening," shared about a trip he had taken to Israel with a group of Inuit at a meeting I "happened" to attend. My daughter was being home schooled, but as a part of her schooling, one day a week she was integrated into a public school.

Her class went on a field trip to the Jewish war museum and confirmed Canada's anti-Semitic actions during WWII. One of the most peculiar things though, was that I kept on seeing geese flying in formation, but instead of flying south, they kept on going east. "Very strange," I thought.

In November, during an intercession meeting at the "It's A New Day" studios in Winnipeg, Kitty had this prayer picture: she saw someone "like Jesus" standing above the earth on a high rock, around Newfoundland. He was facing Canada with a pace stick under His arm—the kind that a marching band conductor uses to set the pace of the band as they walk. The stick had a gold tip. He raised the stick and touched seven different people from across Canada. They then received pace sticks as well, only theirs were silver tipped. Turning around, they then "walked" over the Atlantic. When they came to land, they touched other people, who in turn also received silver tipped pace sticks and joined the rest of the group as they walked. Then they stopped.

Later, I took out a globe and asked, "Kitty, where did they stop? Can you point it out?" Without even looking at the countries, she drew a line with her finger from the east of Canada right to Israel.

"Do you know what country that is?" I asked.

"Nope, haven't a clue," she responded.

"Well, it is Israel," I informed her.

"Cool" she said, "I guess Jesus wants people to go to Israel." And off she bounded. This was BEFORE I had spoken to her about the idea of going to Israel!

Chapter 11 ~ Next Steps

As I was reading my Bible, the Lord brought back the scriptures that He had already used to speak to me:

Do not be afraid, for I am with you; I will bring your children from the east and gather you from the west. I will say to the north, "Give them up!" and to the south, "Do not hold them back." Bring my sons from afar and my daughters from the ends of the earth—everyone who is called by my name, whom I have created for My glory...you are my witnesses. [45]

As I pondered these verses, my mind flashed back to the worship times at Target World in 1996, but this time I had the sense that the time at Target Word was only a picture of what God wanted to do. By now I had a growing sense that God wanted me to take a team of kids to Israel. Reflecting on this scripture, the Lord impressed on me the thought that, while we were there, we were to pray that the Jewish children would come home to Israel from the four corners of the earth.

"Canada is a multicultural nation," I realized, "So maybe we could take people from Canada as representatives of people from the nations. Yeah...and then they could pray for God's glory to fall on the earth as they prayed for their root nation and also for Canada, the place they now call home." These were the kind of thoughts that were flitting around in my head—thoughts that were totally off the radar, or so I thought. So I asked the Lord if He would please confirm them if they were actually His thoughts too.

Section Three

Early in the New Year, I was awakened by a vivid dream. In the dream I heard a voice declare, "It is time!" Then I saw a holy figure standing above the earth over the north of Canada. He had a rod in His hand and raised it. As He lowered it, everything parted before Him—seas of water as well as seas of people when the parting touched the land. Paths were immediately laid from North America, South America and Africa, creating smooth highways as they cut through all sorts of terrain and the sea. They all pointed to Israel. Then a cry resonated, "Go forth. It is time!" In the background I could hear a song begin to swell, and in my spirit, I joined in. It was the song from *Godspell*, "Prepare ye the way of the Lord!" I so wanted to sing along at the top of my lungs.

Shaken, I woke up, and stumbled into the living room.

"Lord, what was that all about?" I prayed. "If this is from You, please show me Your ways. Yes, step by step, please lead me." Trembling, I opened my Bible randomly and, one after the other, scriptures leapt out!

> *A voice is calling,*
> *"Clear the way for the Lord in the wilderness;*
> *Make smooth in the desert a highway for our God.*
> *Let every valley be lifted up,*
> *And every mountain and hill be made low;*
> *And let the rough ground become a plain,*
> *And the rugged terrain a broad valley;*
> *Then the glory of the Lord will be revealed,*
> *And all flesh will see it together..."*
> (Isaiah 40:3–5)

Chapter 11 ~ Next Steps

> *Awake, awake, put on strength, O arm of the Lord;*
> *Awake as in the days of old, the generations of long ago...*
> *Was it not You who dried up the sea,*
> *The waters of the great deep;*
> *Who made the depths of the sea a pathway*
> *For the redeemed to cross over?*
> *So the ransomed of the Lord will return*
> *And come with joyful shouting to Zion,*
> *And everlasting joy will be on their heads...*
> (Isaiah 51:9–11)

> *Listen! Your watchmen lift up their voices,*
> *They shout joyfully together;...*
> *The Lord has bared His holy arm*
> *In the sight of the nations,*
> *That all the ends of the earth may see*
> *The salvation of our God...*
> *Depart, Depart, go out from there,*
> *Touch nothing unclean;*
> *Go out of the midst of her, purify yourselves....*
> *For the Lord will go before you,*
> *And the God of Israel will be your rear guard.*
> (Isaiah 52:8–12)

Humbly I knelt down and said, "God, I really don't understand all of this, but if You would like me to take a team to Israel, I will do so. Only please show me the way."

The next day I phoned David and shared with him what the Lord seemed to be saying. Then I met with our intercessors. ALL felt a strong witness to this plan, and material started to fall into my lap.

I literally didn't have to look for anything; I only had to follow the leads as God gave them. Peg Byars was now acting as administrator for Watchmen and started sending me e-mails with the thoughts the Lord was giving the Watchmen leadership. When visiting Russell in Calgary, I noticed a book on his coffee table, *Exodus II*, by Steve Lightle. As I scanned through the book, I got more and more excited.

"Russ, do you know what this book is all about?"

"Yes," he replied, "it has something to do with God bringing Jewish people home from Russia—the 'North' they call it, I believe."

The book vividly relates the story of how 1,000,000 Jews had returned home from Russia over the previous few years and the miracles that God had orchestrated to prepare the way.

I will say to the north 'give them up.'

"It's happening, God is actually fulfilling the promises that I have been reading about, like NOW. This is AMAZING," I underlined.

"Man, what is God doing?" I asked myself. "O.K. So I really am getting the feeling I am supposed to do this, but if Mexico was scary, and Quebec was way out there, THIS is impossible. How do I lead a team to Israel when I haven't even BEEN there? I have family and work responsibilities, and most of the team will most likely be kids. Lord, have You looked at the news lately? There are all sorts of suicide bombings and..."

"Carolin, just watch me. I will prepare the way for you; just rest in My provision. I will not call you to go

Chapter 11 ~ Next Steps

where I don't lead you. Be not afraid, I go before you. I am in control," the Lord gently reassured me.

I started to hear of more people who had recently been to Israel. One was able to give me the contact information for the King's Kids leaders in Israel. Another good friend, Carol, was heading out in a few days to Israel. She promised to look out for a possible "tour guide." When she came back, she mentioned a lady, Sheila, a Canadian who had immigrated to Israel and was living in Ariel. She worked part time as a tour guide and would consider acting as our point person and guide, but only if her kids, six-year-old Naomi and nine-year-old Ayala, could come along. All were Christians.

Carol and another lady and I met together one evening to ask the Lord if we were missing anything that was on His heart for us to do. All day Carol had the number 1,000 going through her mind, but she didn't have a clue as to why. As we prayed, our hearts were drawn to the 1,000 Jewish children from an internment camp in France who, due to red tape in the government, were denied entrance to Canada in WWII.[46] His presence came upon us strongly and we started to get the idea that we needed to repent for what had been done to these children. Since the team was going to include a number of kids, we asked the Lord to give us a visual to help them understand. Children often need something tangible to understand a difficult concept and thus, to be able to make it their own. The thought that came to mind was that we were to make a cradle and count out 1,000 wheat seeds to symbolize the children. These we could place in sackcloth and lay in the cradle. As we brainstormed about possible material for the cradle, simultaneously we verbalized, "It has to be made out of olive wood, since in scripture the olive tree represents Israel!" We also felt that it should be made without nails or screws as, again, in scripture, items holy to the Lord were made without human instruments.

It was decided that I would go to a lumber store to look for olive wood and ask Doug, who is great at making things out of wood, to make the cradle. Carol would look after the sackcloth and seeds.

At the lumber store, they only had a small amount of olive wood from North Africa, but I brought it home anyways, hoping Doug could work a miracle with it. He was NOT convinced that this would work.

"You want me to make a cradle out of this piece of wood, using no nails, only glue!" he quipped. "Not easy!" he declared, putting the wood down and walking away. Now he was convinced I had a screw loose. A day or so later he came back to me.

"You're serious, aren't you?" he said. We looked at the wood. It really was too small, only big enough for the sides and the bottom of a small cradle. Then the lights went on, "Why not see if we can find some maple wood and make the head and foot pieces out of that? It could symbolize how Canada, represented by the maple wood, is joined together with the olive wood, representing Israel," I suggested.

As he set to fashion it, Doug's heart connected. The end result was beautiful. It even had rockers, like a colonial rocking cradle. As we rocked it gently back and forth, tears came to our eyes. The maple and olive wood grafted together: one.

"It rocks!" we stuttered. "It rocks...just as God would have wanted to rock those children in His arms."

Carol was able to gather the grains of wheat and the sackcloth from a Hutterite community that had a real love for the Jewish people. They prayed and blessed the seeds as they were given.

As we gathered the materials together one afternoon, we clearly saw two rainbows outside the living room window.

Afterwards, we discovered that the day that we had met to pray was the first day of the feast of Shavuot, the time of the wheat harvest. In the Jewish calendar this was June 6th, 2000. During this time the Israelites were to remember the Exodus and to care for the stranger, the orphan, the widow and those that could not care for themselves.

Chapter 12

Gathering the Team

GRADUALLY, THE TEAM started to come together. Once again, the Lord would place possible team members on my heart and, again, He would have gone before me to prepare them. Nine-year-old Rachel Demian, David's daughter, was one. When I called, David shared how God had spoken to them two days prior, showing them that Rachel had a call to missions on her life. As a family, they promised they would pray about this particular possibility, to discern whether this was the right timing for her, and then get back to me. I felt that it was important to have an Arab child on the team as one of the nations represented. A few days later, they called back and yes, this was the next step for her.

Christopher, the grandson of the host of the "It's A New Day" program, was another who came to mind. I was about to call and speak to his parents when I heard from a friend that he had been involved in a serious car accident and had broken his legs.

"I guess that answers that!" I thought.

The same evening, I opened my Bible and Jeremiah 31:8 leapt off the page. "Behold I am bringing them from the north country, And I will gather them from the remote parts of the earth, Among them the blind and *the lame.*"[47]

"God, are you asking me to ask Chris now that he can't walk? Are you saying that You will bring back the 'lame' as well?"

So the next morning, with some fear and trepidation, I called. Not surprisingly, they were initially silent, but asked if they could pray about it and get back to me. An hour later, Christopher's mom called and said, "This is so right; we don't even have to think about it anymore. God has already decided it. My mom has been praying about Chris going to Israel in his thirteenth year and has been saving for it in faith. Chris turns thirteen this summer. Since the accident he is a different kid and God has done a deep work in his heart."

Erica was watching a Christian television program and the words "I have called you to be a witness in Jerusalem" resounded in her ears. Tamara called and said that she had heard about the team and that both she and her mom felt that she was to go. Rachel Doerksen had been in Israel the year before. At the Feast of Tabernacles, God had planted a desire in her heart to "reap the harvest" and to return to Israel. Erica contacted a Jewish family in Vancouver about

Chapter 12 ~ Gathering the Team

their daughter, Naomi, and she was prompted to go. Two others received prophetic words confirming them being a part of the team. If God had gone before us in the last trips, this time He was using a steam shovel to clear the way.

Ruth, her husband, Tuck, and their son Luke all felt to go, and God didn't even have to speak to her in the shower this time! It was their 25th wedding anniversary that summer, and the Lord spoke to them from Isaiah: *"It will no longer be said to you, 'Forsaken,' Nor to your land will it any longer be said, 'Desolate'; But you will be called, 'My delight is in her,' And your land, 'Married'; For the Lord delights in you..."*[48]

This scripture refers to the time when Israel is once again in the Land and Jerusalem is a praise on the earth. As a picture of that, and to celebrate, they felt called to go.

Rebecca, a young Asian who had been on the Train of Tears, followed...along with David and Rhonda Peterson, whose guidance had been so helpful the year before. (Rhonda had also been on the Train.)

On a King's Kids team there are various leadership roles set in place to make sure the team runs smoothly. To give you an idea, there are Family Advisors, usually a couple, who look after the everyday functioning of the team, meals, relationships, birthdays and so on. This is crucial, especially for younger teams. David and Rhonda were indispensable in this.

As I thought about who should fill the adult responsibilities on the team, I was drawn to ask Harvey Katz to consider taking the role of Spiritual Advisor. (The

Lord had prompted him to join the team with his daughter Jessica.) The Spiritual Advisors carry the team before the Lord in prayer and often lead the daily devotionals. They are also to be alert for possible concerns spiritually, in whatever form they might come. Then there is a Program Director, who supervises and often leads an aspect of the ministry expressions of the team. Erica filled this role.

Anyway, soon afterwards, I was reading a book about Israel, and came to this insight. ... *"You'll find that a problem with Jewish surnames. We have been dispersed for so long that the old names have changed across place and time...Cohen could be Cahn in Austria, but it could take the form of Katz in Yiddish."*[49]... *Did you know that Cohen is a derivative of Kohath, the line descended through Moses' brother Aaron? It is through this line that Israel got their High Priests.*[50] So, in light of that, it was possible that Harvey Katz had Levitical roots! What better person could there be to carry the team before the Lord in prayer?

When the team of twenty-four was complete and we looked at the makeup, we discovered:

There were ten children aged 9–15 coming from Canada.

Two children were to join us in Israel, making a total of twelve children, reminiscent of the twelve tribes of Israel.

Besides that, there were nineteen nationalities represented among us, including two Métis kids, six Jewish people, and one Arab girl.

Chapter 12 ~ Gathering the Team

As we looked at the names of the people on the team, we were struck at how God had carefully orchestrated even that. The very names proclaimed what we were to do.

Two had the name of Ruth, and both were gentiles and had red hair. On our flight home, in the *En Route* magazine was an article about redheads. It mentioned in an aside that many of the most prominent anti-Semites had been redheads. Interesting.

The two girls named Naomi were both Jewish. This reminded us of the covenant between Ruth and Naomi, *"Your people will be my people and Your God my God."*[51]

One of the young girl's names in Israel was Ayala, meaning 'let us go up' [...to Jerusalem, in context], the word used to describe the return of the Jewish people to the Land of Israel.

There were two Rachels. The scripture of how "Rachel wept for her children; because they were no more..."[52] came to mind. This surely reflected God's heart as He heard the cries of the children who had died in the concentration camps as well as all the children whose destinies have been aborted.

> *"A voice is heard in Ramah, weeping and great mourning, Rachel weeping for her children and refusing to be comforted, because they are no more."*[53]

There was a Christopher and a Kristy-Anne (who was usually addressed by her nickname, Kitty), whose names mean 'Christ-bearer,' reflecting our mandate to pray for the harvest of souls to the ends of the earth.

Boot Camp Once Again

Remember the "staid" Brethren church where Ruth grew up in...in Montreal?...You got it; they welcomed us with open arms. God had provided the team members and now He went ahead by opening this place to us. If we hadn't clued into it before boot camp started, He underlined it as we were driving to the church. It started pouring—a real downpour! As our windshield wipers struggled to keep up with the rain, puttering down the #2 and #20 highways, we looked out of the car windows and saw...a BRILLIANT RAINBOW FILLING THE SKY A fainter second rainbow bracketed it. Harvey and Jessica, whose flight had been delayed, saw the same rainbow from the plane! There it was once again, God's signature, His covenant blessing.

The start-up date for boot camp was picked to fit around air flight availability in the early part of August. Or so we thought! Later that day, we found out that on the Jewish calendar it was significant for a number of the historical events that had occurred on that day. Among them were:

- The Babylonian army destroyed the Holy Temple in 586 BC.[54]
- Titus and the Roman army destroyed the Holy Temple in 70 AD.
- The first crusades began in 1096 AD.

Chapter 12 ~ Gathering the Team

- World War I was declared in 1914 AD, and in 1942 AD, plans for the annihilation of Jews were drafted, escalating World War II.

That we would start this journey of reconciliation on the very day when in history numerous times incredible atrocities had happened concerning the Jewish people on that very day—as Chuck had said before, this was HUGE. We serve an amazing God!

Boot camp was awesome. From dawn to dusk, we bonded, worshipped, learned more about the nation of Israel and its recent history, learned the choreography pieces we would be doing and—not to forget—ate delicious meals. It was amazing to see how team members, without prior dialogue, had received the same confirming scriptures before coming to boot camp. Among them were scriptures which spoke of preparing a highway, raising a standard of righteousness[55] and praying "Your Kingdom come." Tuck had received a prophetic dream about attending a funeral where he was seeking a safe place for some children, but ended up watching the funeral of a young child wrapped in purple and gold cloth. He knew nothing of the cradle story.

However, we needed for the rest of the kids to hear from the Lord as well so that they would know this was for them and take ownership of it. This happened. During a time of waiting on the Lord, the children brought up some of the same thoughts and that somehow we needed to have a way to remember the 1,000 children and have a proper "funeral."

Section Three

I shared with the team the thoughts we had had about the cradle and the wheat. Immediately they connected with and embraced the idea. As we gathered around the cradle on the hardwood basement floor of the church, the ten children decided to each count out 100 grains of wheat from the glass jar of seeds and place them in the sackcloth. You could have heard a pin drop as they knelt, concentrating on their task and its significance. When the seeds had been placed into the sackcloth, Rachel and Rebecca wrapped them up, carefully placing them in the cradle as a mother would lovingly care for her child. (These two girls "just happened" to have the same names as the wives of Isaac and Jacob, the first mothers of Israel). We then prayed that God would bring back to Israel a hundredfold for those who had died.

The three young adult leaders then took a Canadian flag that had been on the Train of Tears and an Israeli flag from Steve Lightle's "Exobus" ministry (a ministry that was helping Russian Jewish orphan children "come back" to Israel). Together, they gently covered the cradle as if they were tucking the children in. Particularly poignant was that, during the counting of the wheat, Tuck quietly went to the car and brought in a CD with a song that fit SO perfectly...Michael W Smith's song, "I Know Your Name."[56]

God moved among us powerfully, instilling in our hearts a profound sense of brokenness.

Chapter 12 ~ Gathering the Team

Kristalnacht

Once again, just like on the Quebec trip in 1998, we experienced spiritual opposition. On that trip, it came in the form of foot injuries. This time, it came in the form of an attack on our car.

One beautiful sunny morning we woke up and went to our vans, planning to do a prayer walk in the Jewish neighbourhood of Montreal. We went to our vans, only to find that the windows of my blue mini-van had been smashed. When he saw it, Harvey immediately gasped, "Kristallnacht!" and with a heavy spirit, turned and went back into the church. I had no idea what he was speaking about. I found out later that he was referring to *"the 'Night of Broken Glass,' the name given to the violent anti-Jewish pogrom of November 9 and 10, 1938. Instigated primarily by Nazi party officials and the SA (Nazi Storm Troopers), the pogrom occurred throughout Germany... and heralded a new wave of anti-Jewish legislation,"*[57] just prior to WWII.

As we viewed the damage and recognized our subsequent fear and feelings of violation, we realized that God had allowed us to feel in microcosm the fear and violation that the Jewish people had felt, and thus, to identify with them to a greater degree. Once again, we realized the significance of this journey and called David and Peg, who immediately sent out even more requests for prayer cover for the team.

Kitty had the impression of a large map of Canada. Superimposed on it in the centre was the star of David and a cross. A short while later she saw a large teardrop fall on the map and watched as it spread all over Canada. A drop of red blood followed and mingled with the water and turned the map red. She then saw the map rise up out of the water and blood but this time it was solid gold. She said, "Because many people have been repenting for the sins in Canada and have cried about it, God will forgive and His glory is going to cover the land."

~

On the Sunday we left Montreal to go to Israel, we presented some musical numbers at St. Stephen's Church. Naomi, a gifted dancer, choreographed an amazing dance that captured the heart of our prayers, performed to the song from the movie *The Prince of Egypt*, titled, "When You Believe."[58]

> *Many nights we prayed, with no proof anyone could hear*
> *In our hearts a hopeful song, we barely understood*
> *Now we are not afraid, although we know there's much to fear*
> *We were moving mountains long before we knew we could*
> *There can be miracles, when you believe*
> *Though hope is frail, it's hard to kill*
> *Who knows what miracles, you can achieve,*
> *When you believe, somehow you will*
> *You will when you believe.*

Chapter 12 ~ Gathering the Team

We also sang a beautiful round in Hebrew from the book of Lamentations:

Hashivenu hashivenu Adonai elecha
Vena shuva, Vena shuva
Chadesh chadesh, yamenu kekedem[59]

(Restore us to Thee, O Lord, that we may be restored. Renew our days as of old.[60])

After the service, we gathered together for lunch in—you guessed it—the parish room at the back of St. Stephen's Church. Looking around at the beautiful wood paneled walls and out the window facing the street, I was drawn back once again to the time when, a year-and-a-half earlier, Erica had given me David Demian's tape. Then further back, I could still visualize the kids horsing around and singing in this very room before they quieted down to hear what was on the hearts of some of Montreal's Christian leaders. Now, once again, we had come to the place of listening and preparing our hearts before God. What was in store? Had God brought this small team together for such a time as this?

Michael Gertsman, a rabbi from Montreal, spoke to us about the importance of going in humility. He shared that, due to years of persecution, the Jewish people might view us with suspicion, so we needed to plant seeds of love. He suggested that we pray that God would sprinkle clean water on their hearts and remove their hearts of stone. He assured us that God would open the way for us and then prayed the Aaronic blessing over us in Hebrew:

Y'va-reh'ha Adonai v'uish-m'reha.
Ya-eyr Adonai panav eyle-ha vihu-neka.
Yoda Adonai panav eyle-ha v'ya-seym l'shalom

The L-rd Bless you and Keep you,
The L-rd make His face shine upon you.
The L-rd lift up his countenance upon you,
and give you peace.[61]

Paul Hawkins, the same fellow who had encouraged us in Atlanta four years prior, then phoned and, on the speaker phones, prayed over the team and blessed us. He said:

There is a witness that this is of God and that He has handpicked each person on the team. The things God spoke to you in preparation be careful to remember, and follow every step in obedience. Unity is very important; don't let anything, however small, come between you and another team member. As overseer of King's Kids, I commission this team and call on the wind, oil and fire anointing to be released. Pray that you will hear God's voice hour after hour, and respond immediately. You are laying down your lives, not literally, but for God's purposes in Canada. I pray for angels now to surround you on the journey there and the journey back here.

~

Chapter 12 ~ Gathering the Team

In England, on our stopover, God once again answered prayer by providing us a place to rest. I had been so concerned that we not get overtired. Anyone who does a lot of international travel will know how gruelling it can be. We had just endured a nine-hour flight, starting at the end of the day, followed now by a fourteen-hour layover, and then another eight-hour flight arriving at the start of the day. This just didn't seem like a good thing. Rhonda was able to make connections beforehand with some friends at Holy Trinity Brompton Church in London. They kindly offered to provide lunch and a place to rest. When we arrived, bleary eyed and yawning, we noticed that the room had about twenty-five huge beanbags on the floor. Immediately, the kids (well, not only the kids) let out a "wheeee" and plopped down. Some of the kids fell asleep mid-sentence. All of us slept for about four hours and then took time to sightsee. I stayed behind with the luggage and just lay down to "read and pray." The last thing I remember was.... Well, anyways, I woke up I don't know how much later as the rest of the team stomped into the room.

"Where were you? Are you o.k.? We pounded on the door and called your name but no one answered. So we had to go out back to get the caretaker to open the door!"

I had not heard a thing. In a fog, I looked up at them, feeling very foolish. This was unusual for me, as I wake up if a fly walks across the ceiling.

"I will give you the land and I will give you rest, remember?" I heard the Lord whisper in my ear. All that fretting for nothing!

With renewed energy and focus, we ate lunch and had a time of prayer with the people at the church who had hosted us. We prayed for England, that God would bless her. The church we were at was the church which had started the Alpha ministry. Harvey had so wanted to connect with the Alpha ministry while in England and, as I had not been aware of the place we were to go, having left that detail to Rhonda, now he was ecstatic. We finished our time of prayer by singing "The Lord's Prayer," and on the last note the church bells started to ring.

Chapter 13

Israel

THE PLANE ROLLED to a stop at the designated spot, about a hundred yards from the terminal of the Ben Gurion Airport. Pumped, we could hardly wait to get off the plane. The doors opened, but the line moved at an agonizingly slow pace. When at last we got to the door and erupted into the open air, we were greeted with the warm moist air of the Mediterranean. As it was only five in the morning, it was barely light outside. THIS was the land that Jesus walked! Most of us paused as we took in this moment, trying to capture as much as possible in this first glance while the younger kids ran around, glad to stretch their legs.

As we gathered our bags, Sheila, our "tour guide," and her daughters materialized, little Naomi excitedly jumping around the team.

"I'm Nomi," she declared, with a grin that was missing a front tooth, "and this is Ayala!" Hugs and introductions were shared all around as Sheila went on to explain that she had been able to get us a bus, but not what we had asked. We had asked for a half sized bus with a driver.

"There are a lot of small tour groups right now and the only bus available was a full sized air conditioned bus."

My heart both sank and soared.

"Humm, how much extra will that be?" I asked cautiously.

"Oh, nothing. It was their miscalculation!"

Tears filled my eyes once again as I looked at the bus and the team. "This is amazing; everyone is here and with an AIR-conditioned bus, to boot!"

"Yay God!" Carol exclaimed, pumping her fist in the air. During the next ten days we realized what a gift it really was, with the temperature being in the mid-thirties most of the time.

God had done it. We were in Israel, the team had all arrived safely and there really was a Sheila at the end of the e-mails. Wiping at the tears of joy, I thought, "I really should carry along some Kleenex; this is getting to be a habit."

After we stored the luggage and props underneath, we clambered onto the bus and headed for our first destination: Arni and Yonit Klein's "house of prayer" in Tel Aviv.

A few days before I left Winnipeg, I had realized that we didn't have a confirmed place to stay on our first day in Israel. The place that we had lined up had fallen through at the last minute. I fired off an e-mail to Peg, asking her to pray and to contact David Demian, as he had some other connections in Israel.

Chapter 13 ~ Israel

Early in the morning the following day I phoned, forgetting that it was six in the morning there, and a lady answered the phone. When I asked her if David had somehow had any luck finding a place for us, she replied, "No. I haven...sorry, can you hold on a minute? The other phone is ringing!" She placed me on hold. A second later she picked up the phone and exclaimed, "Wait a minute, David is on the other line. I will connect you two!" After excited greetings were exchanged, he told me that there was a new house of prayer starting in Tel Aviv and they would be pleased to have us come as their first guests.

So now, barely two weeks later, we were graciously received in the large limestone foyer of the house of prayer and escorted up winding stars to the upper rooms of the house. Kindly, they pointed us to the rooms where we would be staying and, once again, we crashed for a few hours. When we woke, they invited us to join them for a time of worship in the prayer room.

In their worship centre there were beautiful coloured banners, each one with a name of one of the tribes of Israel, displayed all around the room. A talented team of musicians was leading the worship. It didn't take long for the Lord's presence to fall in the place, and even though we were tired, we joined in for three-and-a-half hours. From song to song we entered in and prayed with one another as we sensed God drawing us closer to Himself. A number of the kids whispered, "Did you feel it? It is just as if we are being ROCKED in God's arms." All we knew was that this was a safe place, and often during our time in Israel, we reflected on this experience.

The next morning, we woke up to Tuck whistling the lullaby that Chuck had sung to us before we went to bed during boot camp: "My heart wants to know, yes, my heart wants to know everything's alright." Overnight Peg had sent us an e-mail with a word that one of the intercessors had received for us. She was shown a picture of the Lord holding the team cradled and safe in His hands, hands that were red with His blood. The scripture she was given was Ezra 8:31, which says:

> *Then we journeyed...to go to Jerusalem; and the hand of our God was over us, and He delivered us from the hand of the enemy and the ambushes by the way.*

This was amazing, considering the kids' thoughts of the previous evening. But also, as two days before, Tuck and Carol, who had flown in on a direct flight from Canada, had the tires blow out in the car that they were driving en route to Sheila's home. They walked away unharmed.

We shared this with the team over a delicious breakfast of tomatoes, cucumbers, boiled eggs and flat bread, which we would come to realize was very common fare in Israel. As we dialogued back and forth, we knew we were to share the story of the cradle with Yonit and Arni and a few of their intercessors. Tuck, who was often seen cradling and rocking it in His arms, had actually carried the cradle that way

Chapter 13 ~ Israel

from Canada on his flight. He now took it out and carefully placed it on the floor in the centre of the conference room we were gathered in. Together as a team we shared the story. We expressed our desire, as children of all ages, to stand in the gap and repent on behalf of Canada for turning away these children. Nine-year-old Rachel Demian pinned the "Never Again" pin from the Winnipeg Gathering on the sackcloth wrapped around the 1,000 grains of wheat that represented the children. As she did she started weeping. Rhonda placed the prayer shawl over her shoulders as others joined in...Rachel weeping for her children who were not.

There was not a dry eye present. The words of the scripture "Comfort, O Comfort My people"[62] were powerfully expressed at one point, when David Peterson started playing a beautiful lament on his violin. For a long while we were silent.

One of the intercessors who had joined us that morning said, "I didn't think God could touch my heart like this. It would be really good if you took this cradle with you wherever you go and share it, as God leads you, to soften our hard hearts." Interestingly, one of the kids, Amy, had a picture of a stone wall the day before with a tear falling on it. We mentioned this to her and she affirmed, "That was me, my last name is Stone and my heart was as well. Your tears have softened my heart."

> *Therefore say, "Thus says the Lord God, 'I will gather you from the peoples and assemble you out*

> *of the countries among which you have been scattered, and I will give you the land of Israel.'...And I will give them one heart, and put a new spirit within them. And I will take the heart of stone out of their flesh and give them a heart of flesh, that they may walk in My statutes and keep My ordinances and do them Then they will be my people, and I shall be their God."*[63]

~

We also wanted to share about what God had put on our hearts concerning the mandate we felt to call back the "children of Israel" from the four corners of the earth. We shared information from the documentary we had watched during boot camp, "The Ten Lost Tribes," by Simcha Jacobovici, a documentary filmmaker who had spent four years seeking the lost tribes of Israel. He had made a persuasive argument that the people he had interviewed in the film were indeed the modern-day descendants of the lost tribes of Israel. He was the first journalist to document that these isolated groups shared some beliefs and customs that are extremely similar to Jewish practices. This documentary "just happened" to be aired on television prior to boot camp.

We felt that the ten children from Canada who had joined the two children in Israel were a picture of what God wanted to do, bringing the two into one.[64] He portrays this image in Ezekiel 37 by the miracle of two sticks—one representing Ephraim, and the other Judah—becoming one. Unity is very important to

Chapter 13 ~ Israel

God, as is making sure that His original covenant purposes are fulfilled.

After we shared this, Arni got up and said, "I have something for you guys." He came back a few minutes later, carrying a number of native drums—twelve of them, to be exact. I had heard about these drums. The summer before, a King's Kids team from Calgary had gone to a YWAM base called "Eagle's Nest." While there, the kids had been handed drums to use in prayer. They were beautifully crafted, but what was interesting was that on each one was written the name of one of the tribes of Israel in Hebrew script.

Earlier in the year, I had remarked to one of the other team members about how neat it would be if we could take some drums like that—each one dedicated to the Lord—to Israel. I even went so far as to call the Eagle's Nest base to ask if they knew where the drums were. They had no idea. Well, here they were, the very same drums taken to Israel by Linda Prince earlier in the year and left at Arni's place. What were the "chances" of that happening?

Quietly, Arni handed them out to the children: twelve drums, twelve kids, a visual and tactile prayer tool to help them pray. (The youngest child received the drum with Benjamin's name.) As we played these drums we called out the names of the various tribes. After the time of repentance we had just had, it was a time of release and we felt we were free to call out to the North, South, East and West. It was AWESOME!

Watchmen on the hills shout out,
Open wide the gate
For the Lord has called us back,
It's time to celebrate.
It's time to build and plant
And gather in the fruit,
Join your hands and dance
To the sound of strings and flute!
Restrain your voice from weeping
And your eyes from their tears,
Jesus our deliverer has redeemed the broken years.
So dance with all that's in you,
Shout to all the earth,
O Lord save your people,
Gather them to yourself.[65]

~

A full couple of days walking in the Land

From Tel Aviv we went to Shiloh, where Samuel had been dedicated. Climbing up a wooden outlook platform, we could see for miles over the hills and valleys. Here and there olive trees popped out of the dry earth. As we looked around, we realized that rain was indeed a need in this land and so we proceeded to sing "Mayim Mayim," an upbeat Hebrew song praying for rain. The kids loved this song and would often spontaneously erupt into singing it. It is the kind of song that, when you can't get to sleep at night, lingers and keeps you awake even more. However, Mayim aside, it was mind boggling to think that at this very site so much history had played out. Here, at the start of our trek through the land, we became linked to what had been spoken years before. We prayed as Samuel did: "Speak, Lord, for your servant is listening.[66] Show us what is on your heart and help us to be obedient like Samuel was."

Shechem, the site of one of the few modern day Samaritan communities, is also located on what is known as the Mount of Blessing. Here we read passages from Deuteronomy, asking God to remember His covenant promise of blessing to the Jewish people. In doing so, we recognized once again the Holiness of God and how serious He is that we choose life. We also asked Him to bless the Samaritan people who had been supportive of the Israelis and the Palestinian people who had a village in-between the "Mountain of Blessing" and the "Mountain of Cursing." We each placed a stone in a pile at the site as a memorial.

We were awestruck to think that long ago, at this very site, the tribes of Israel had stood, reciting the blessings and curses that would befall them in obedience or disobedience to God's word.

Moses spoke to the people, saying:

This day the Lord your God commands you to observe these statutes and judgments; therefore you shall be careful to observe them with all your heart and with all your soul. Today you have proclaimed the Lord to be your God, and that you will walk in His ways and keep His statutes, His commandments, and His judgments, and that you will obey His voice. Also today the Lord has proclaimed you to be His special people, just as He promised you, that you should keep all His commandments, and that He will set you high

> *above all nations which He has made, in praise, in name, and in honor, and that you may be a holy people to the Lord your God, just as He has spoken.* (Deuteronomy 26:16–19 NKJV)

> *...I have set before you life and death, blessing and cursing; therefore choose life, that both you and your descendants may live; that you may love the Lord your God, that you may obey His voice, and that you may cling to Him, for He is your life and the length of your days; and that you may dwell in the land which the Lord swore to your fathers, to Abraham, Isaac, and Jacob, to give them.* (Deuteronomy 30:19–20 NKJV)

~

Our next destination was the Mount Carmel range of mountains. Such a contrast to the dry areas around Shiloh and Shechem! These were beautiful lush green hills covered with dense trees. Here and there we spotted caves in the mountain face.

We stayed in the area at the beautiful "Elijah House," a centre for prayer and worship surrounded by flowering trees. In the back was a cute pathway where we could enjoy the quiet. Bamboo-type chairs with colourful cushions were scattered in the nooks and crannies along the path for that purpose. Laughter filled the halls after supper as we debriefed, and each small group creatively shared their thoughts.

In the morning, we met in the prayer centre they called "Elijah's Cave." Fittingly, it was in the basement of their chapel, which was made of the same white

Chapter 13 ~ Israel

limestone that seemed so prevalent wherever you went in Israel. A wall surrounded the recessed room and a candled menorah flickered softly. We had come from Canada to bless Israel. In the same way, we wanted to pray for Canada from this location in Israel—that God would bless our nation and challenge her to "choose this day whom you will serve"[67] just as Elijah had challenged Israel to do millennia before.

To do so we worshipped along with "Break Dividing Walls," a March for Jesus CD, and prayed for God to break down the divisions between people groups and provinces, asking that God's glory would fill our nation. We joined hands, called out the nations that were represented by our team and prayed for unity—that God would prepare Canada to be a blessing and healer to the nations.

One of the girls who had Mohawk roots, Ashley, donned her Native dress and danced to the "Mohawk Chant" on the tape that called for the Holy Spirit to fill the land. As she knelt down with James, we prayed for the healing of the Aboriginal people—covering them both with Canada's flag—and poured oil, a symbol of healing, all over it. She broke down in tears and travail, seeming to carry a deep burden for the Aboriginal children in Canada.

We then prayed, "Canada, chose today who you will serve! As the writing over the doorway of the parliament buildings in Ottawa proclaims, we ask, Lord, that You WILL have dominion from sea to sea."[68]

From the Elijah House we went to the site where Elijah confronted the prophets of Baal. There, on the

Section Three

roof of a building, the kids sensed that they were to pray for the nations once again, facing outwards in a circle. James and Rachel both had an impression of a huge hand throwing out kernels of wheat. We had grain left over after counting the 1,000 seeds for the cradle, so the kids threw out handfuls of wheat over the railing of the balcony into the valley. They prayed that the seeds they threw would represent the seed that fell on good soil and yield hundredfold fruit.

The site looked over the Jezreel Valley, a lush green valley covered with trees. Much later, we learned that Jezreel means 'God sows,' the scripture referring to the time when God would once more "plant"[69] the Jewish people into the land of Israel.

> ...*And they will respond to Jezreel. I will plant her for myself in the land; I will show my love to the one I called "Not my loved one." I will say to those called "Not my people," "You are my people"; and they will say, "You are my God." (Hosea 2:22–23 NIV)*

~

One day, both Christopher and Kristy-Anne were hurt. Out of the blue, Kitty fell over backwards and landed on her back on a sharp rock. It was very fortunate that she was wearing a backpack that caught the blow. While Chris was doing a flip in the Sea of Galilee, his face and knee collided with a whack, which knocked out a part of a tooth and bruised his nose. Later, when we arrived at the place we were to stay overnight, there was disagreement about the time of arrival and confusion about the accommodations. That night some of us were ready to go home.

However, in the morning during a time of prayer with the leaders of the team, the Lord showed us what was happening. Harvey reminded us that, the day before, we had been praying at the site of the confrontation between the prophets of Baal and the prophets of God. He felt that what we were experiencing was a letdown just like Elijah experienced. Harvey and some of the other staff confessed that they, too, were discouraged. He also reminded us that Tiberius is especially resistant to the Gospel and said, "If you tried to preach here you would not be welcomed." Suddenly I understood. The two children who had been injured were the ones whose names meant 'Follower of Christ' or 'Christ-bearer.'

Shortly afterwards, we had a time of worship and I asked the kids if they were discouraged or had sensed anything unusual. None of them had noticed anything unusual. God had kept them safe. We shared with them a bit of what we felt had been going on and, in response, sang the song "Children of Light," declaring who we are and encouraging one another to "let our lights shine."

We challenged each one once again to make sure that there were no possible loopholes, and re-read the prayer that Paul Hawkins had prayed over the team. We had daily had a time of making sure there was no offence, but on the day when both injuries occurred, there had been an altercation between two of the team members. It was nothing major, but it was there. Ruth had laid out the lunches on the table and had asked the kids to wait until everyone was ready and to have a word of prayer before we ate. One of the kids ignored the directive and grabbed a handful of chips. As he was being challenged about this attitude, Kristy-Anne fell over backwards.

The object lesson showed us how serious God is about us walking in unity and laying down our rights for each another, even in the small things. This was a turning point for the team, as we all saw HOW important unity truly is.

~

The following day on the shores of the Sea of Galilee, we met with an Israeli King's Kids team, an exuberant group of young people. We shared the story of the cradle with them, and again, it was very well received. One young man tearfully prayed in Hebrew over the team for a long time. Seeing how deeply this touched him, we wondered what his background was. Afterwards, they shared with us some of the ministries they were involved in, thus further connecting the hearts of the two teams.

Watching the kids start to wiggle and fidget, being beckoned by the sun glittering off the Sea of Galilee, we brought an end to the "serious stuff." The teams embraced and in no time at all raced, albeit somewhat gingerly, to the water and plunged in. The stones on the beach were a bit painful to walk on, but that was a

Chapter 13 ~ Israel

small price to pay compared to the thrill of actually being there. Giggling and laughter ensued as we splashed each other and ate the picnic lunch that had been provided. Amy later recalled a highlight of the trip being covering herself from head to toe with the mud from the sea! Go figure!

~

I received an e-mail from one of the team members who had been involved in our outreach to Mexico. He was on an outreach to China and a line in his letter was quite amusing. "The drivers here are a breed apart - lanes exist only for the sheer purpose of decorating the grey pavement and the wanton disregard for oncoming traffic, pedestrians and cyclists is something to behold, if you aren't already cringing in the backseat with your head between your legs."[70] It reminded me of the driving in Israel and I thought, "The drivers here must go to the same driving school as they do in China...and Mexico...and as I remember, in Quebec, where they even have signs that say, 'Wait for the green light'!"

Sigh...in Winnipeg, Manitoba, we are known for our orderly driving—all the same speed, you can't pass anyone and everyone gets there the same time, no matter where you're going—not very exciting. Our Israeli bus driver, Simcha, (whose name means 'joy') manoeuvred impossible turns down steep mountains and even made a U-turn right over a sidewalk without blinking an eye!

As for the food, well, falafel and more falafel and cucumbers and tomatoes and boiled eggs is what we will remember. If we ever have a team reunion, it will not be complete without our drippy falafels, eaten on the street corner in the 38-degree Celsius sun. Mind you, they were probably healthy—made from chickpeas and all sorts of vegetables and topped with a nondescript sauce of three possible colour choices. You could have the option of having fries added to the sandwich (for westerners, I'm sure). Fries in a Pita...whatever...

BUT on the way home we saw a fast food restaurant at the airport in England. Guess what we had as a treat to help re-entry? Wouldn't you know it? A quarter of the team felt nauseous afterwards—one even threw up. Sigh...guess we should have stuck to falafels.

Chapter 14

Stones Laid Down ... and Removed

BACK IN WINNIPEG before the start of the outreach, as I pondered the initial visions the Lord gave us concerning this mission, an idea started to form. I sensed that the Lord was calling the team to go into the Jordan River and, from there, to call the Jewish people home from the four corners of the earth. As time passed, another thought grew. It was that we were to symbolically "call forth" from the four corners of the earth both the harvest and the labourers to go into the harvest. However, I strongly sensed that I was to keep this hidden until the time we were actually in the Jordan. I did, however, share it with a few intercessors so they could cover us in prayer as we did. As confirmation that these thoughts were from the Lord, I asked Him to send me rocks from the four corners of the earth and from the four corners of Canada to be laid as an altar in the Jordan at the right time.

Section Three

A short time later, I received a parcel from Nunavut in the mail. "What could this be, I wondered? I wasn't expecting anything."

I opened the box and found the following letter from a Doug Willoughby. He mentioned that he was a friend of Roger Armbruster, who had led a team of Inuit people to Israel the previous year.

Enclosed is the rock you prayed for. I asked the Lord to show me the rock to send when I went for my inspection tour of the mine underground on Tuesday. The first location I went to had nice ore samples, but the miners were busy loading trucks in the area and I couldn't stay long enough to get a sample. The second place had some nice crystals, but the miner was drilling in the area and I couldn't stay there either. The third place was a waste drift, so I wasn't expecting any rock specimens there. As I was leaving, a brilliant crystal shone from the floor. I walked over to where the light was but I couldn't find the crystal. I looked up at the wall and saw the largest single pyrite crystal I have ever seen. Unfortunately, it was too high on the wall to reach. I looked on the floor below and found a toaster sized ore specimen with excellent crystals. I broke this piece up by hitting it against a sharp rock and retrieved a good specimen.

It was found in the Nanisivik Mine, a lead/silver/zinc mine, in one of the most northerly and deepest areas of the mine. The mine is located near the northern tip of Baffin Island in the High Arctic north of 73 N and 84 west and about 550 miles north of the Arctic circle. It is about 32 km NE of

Chapter 14 ~ Stones Laid Down...and Removed

Arctic Bay. Nanisivik is Canada's 3rd most Northerly community.

I must have mentioned my hope for these stones to Roger Armbruster who, in turn, passed it on. I couldn't help but reflect on the significance of the fact that the first stone came from the Inuit people, who have made such a profound connection with the Israeli people.

The stone itself was a GORGEOUS stone with silver flakes all over it. The silver was interesting in two ways: first, because it related to my daughter's impression of Jesus standing on a rock facing Canada, pointing out seven people, each of whom were given silver tipped pace sticks, who in turn followed Him across the Atlantic to Israel. Then also because in Isaiah it speaks of the return of the Jewish people from afar, bringing their gold and silver.[71]

The second stone came from New Zealand. In May I received a YWAM International poster about the Hui 2000 conference. The poster said that *"...you will cross the Jordan here to go in and take possession of the land the Lord your God is giving you...From around the world, God is gathering us together to lead us across the Jordan as we rediscover the destiny of our mission for the next forty years."*

When I read that, something in me leapt. Here we were, planning to literally go to the Jordan with people who had roots in the nations of the world. We were planning to be there about ten days before the conference started in New Zealand, and a word had already been given to the team that ours would be a forerunning team. Joanne Gannoka, who had previously been on the King's Kids team with Dave and Rhonda Peterson in 1995, sent the stone from New Zealand. The stone came from the site of the original venue of the YWAM conference. When looking at the stone, a few intercessors pointed out that there was a slightly raised part of the stone in the shape of an eagle. Our team T shirts had an eagle leading a flock of Canada Geese, reminiscent of the scripture in Exodus 19:4 of how He bore the children of Israel home on eagles' wings. Also on the shirt was a maple tree, over which was the rainbow. The last Canada goose in formation carried a red maple leaf from that tree. This was to point to the scripture "the leaves of the tree are for the healing of the nations."[72]

The next stone was from China. It was sent to me by a lady on a King's Kids team, "the road to China." She picked it up after a prayer time on top of a mountain 15,000 feet above sea level. Shaped like an arrow head, the stone represented "overcomes" to her.

Tamara contributed the last stone. She picked it up on a beach on the west side of Vancouver Island, close to the site of a UN peacekeeping base.

That gave us the stones from the four corners of the earth, but we needed two more from Canada: the western stone being the stone from Vancouver Island, and the northern stone being the one from Nunavut.

The year before, Ruth Williams brought two stones from the most southerly place in Canada, Point Pelee, for the altar of remembrance at the Gathering. For

Chapter 14 ~ Stones Laid Down...and Removed

some reason, she left one of the stones on a shelf in our basement. I noticed it lying there, and when I realized where it was from, I brought it along.

My husband brought the stone from the east home after being at a conference in Montreal. He had been sitting next to a lady at supper time and had "happened" to mention that I was looking for a rock from the east. He didn't go into a lot of details. However, she piped up, "Well you can't get much further east in Canada then Cape Spears in Newfoundland. By the way, I was just there and picked up a rock. You can have it!" She dug it out of her purse and gave it to him.

As I mentioned earlier, I had only shared the idea of the stones and the Jordan River with a few intercessors. I did share it with Paul Hawkins, whom we had met in the prayer tent in Atlanta, when he "just happened" to be in Winnipeg for a TV taping. We met with him and he strongly encouraged us to continue seeking the Lord, especially about the idea of praying for the harvest. With all this preparation, where was God leading us?

~

So, when we came to Israel, I asked Sheila if she knew of a spot where we could go into the Jordan River and pray. Offhand she couldn't think of anything, and when she conferred with Simcha, he couldn't think of any place either. It was now halfway through our time in Israel and we had just finished our meeting with the King's Kids team at the Galilee. The next day we were heading inland to Jerusalem, so it was now or never. I didn't think that the Lord had led us this far not to take us to the Jordan and accomplish what He had put on our hearts.

As we climbed onto the bus, I once again approached both Sheila and Simcha, stressing that I really felt that it was important for us to go into the Jordan River that day. Once again they both drew a blank, Simcha confirming, "Well, the river is too deep—over three metres in most places around here. The only direct access is in the Jordan Valley in the nation of Jordan, and you can't access the river there for political reasons. However, there is a spot not too far from here where there is a bridge that crosses the Jordan. We could cross there, I suppose. Any other location has a lot of bulrushes and bugs and the access is too steep and rocky."

I had to go along with what they said. However, knowing this was very important, I decided that we would go to the site close to the bridge and have a look for ourselves. As we drove, we prayed that the Lord would clear the way. After we crossed the bridge, we got out of the bus and walked downhill towards the river through a path strewn with thorn bushes until we came to a little clearing high up on the bank of the river. Some local kids were fly fishing there, but yes, it was steep and rocky and there was no place to climb down or to stand in the river there.

Backtracking to the clearing, we stopped and sat down. There I shared the story of the rocks and the sense of what I thought God wanted us to do as a

Chapter 14 ~ Stones Laid Down...and Removed

team. Together we prayed that God would lead us to the right place. Then Rhonda piped up, "God gave us that very scripture about crossing the Jordan when we started with King's Kids nearly ten years ago. This is so significant for YWAM/King's Kids right now. I know this is from the Lord, so let's all pray."

"Father, you are an awesome God! You have brought us to this place at this time for a reason. You made the rivers and the land, so please show us where to go. This wasn't our idea, but Yours, and we want to do what You asked us to do."

So we started walking again, not really knowing where we were going, and it was SO hot: 37 degrees Celsius and sunny. No one complained. After about half an hour we came upon a site where some people looked like they were attempting to raft down the river. It didn't look too steep. Prayerfully, we asked the Lord, "Is this the place?" but the kids just didn't feel right about it. It was noisy and there were too many people.

As we caught our breath in the shade of some weeping willow type trees, Tuck quietly went off on his own and a short while later came back with, "I think I found a place." About 100 yards away in the bush a path led to the edge of the Jordan. The water was only a foot or so deep and easily accessible. There was a grassy area with a very small beach surrounded by tall grasses. It was quiet and private and, as we gathered at the spot, I was overwhelmed. PERFECT!

Sheila couldn't believe it. "I never knew this was here!" she exclaimed.

"Yeah, but God did," I smiled.

In the book of Joshua we read that the priests stepped into the Jordan first and the people crossed in afterwards.[73] Now, we were not going to re-enact what happened there, but we thought that Harvey was to stand on one side, representing Israel, and Dave and Rhonda, representing YWAM, were to stand on the other side as the team went into the Jordan between them.

The two aboriginal kids walked in first, hand in hand. The rest of the team followed, worshipping as they went. Some threw out handfuls of wheat in all directions, "calling in" the harvest. As the Lord led each of us individually, we consecrated ourselves as workers in the harvest. Together we asked the Lord to send out more missionaries to the four corners of the earth, calling out nations as we did. Finally, we asked the Lord to continue to bring home the children of Israel from the four corners of the earth.

Standing in the Jordan, with the bulrushes waving gently in the breeze and the sun reflecting off the water, we laid the stones down in the water at the edge of the Jordan. We had not thought beforehand about how to build the altar, but in one accord, we all felt it was to be in the water, hidden. Then Rachel sang from the shore overlooking the altar, surrounded by bulrushes:

Here by the water we'll build an altar to praise You, from the rocks that we brought here... Knowing You can make them Holy...[74]

Chapter 14 ~ Stones Laid Down...and Removed

While she was singing, a dove landed on the shore opposite us. It seemed to rest patiently the entire time she was singing and then took off again...just as she finished.

~

From there we headed off to Jerusalem—the holy city at last! The heat was incredible, and we were SO thankful for the air-conditioned bus. Carol kept us supplied with water bottles and we sang, as only a busload of pumped people can, "Mayim, Mayim, Mayim." As we drove down the highway through the Jordan Valley, we saw miles and miles of bleak stony wilderness. Then suddenly, opposite the city of Jericho, lush green fields appeared. Banana trees and other fruit trees lined the road for miles and miles. Alongside the trees were pipes with desalinated water carried in from the Mediterranean Sea—"The desert shall blossom."[75] The contrast was amazing.

As we looked at the terrain between Jericho and Jerusalem, the Bedouin tents and the occasional goat or camel, we realized it was another world. The parable of the man traveling from Jerusalem to Jericho was vividly impressed on our minds.

Then, as dusk was falling, we came over the hill—Jerusalem! The many lights reflected off the white limestone buildings and the city gleamed with a golden hue. Breathtaking. The next few days were a dream. We walked the narrow cobblestone streets of the old city and ate bagels in one of the numerous sidewalk cafes. Browsing in the colourful market, we learned how to barter. We prayed at the western wall, the site of the old temple, and left prayers from friends and family at home in the nooks and crannies of the Kotel, joining the thousands that had been placed there before. We were amazed at the height and size of the massive stones that comprised the wall and later learned that the largest weighed 570 tons, the heaviest object ever to have been lifted by man without the aid of machinery.[76]

But what caught our eyes most were the people: squirming children holding their parents hands; IDF soldiers in their Khaki uniforms keeping a watchful eye from the vantage point of the shade of surrounding trees; Orthodox Jews, heads covered by their prayer shawl or tallit, rocking back and forth, praying in Hebrew earnestly seeking the God of Abraham Isaac and Jacob.

For two of the days in Jerusalem we stayed at Tom Hess's house of prayer on the Mount of Olives. As we looked out across Jerusalem from the flat part of the roof of the house, we danced and sang with others from the nations who had joined us there, declaring: "Your Kingdom come, Your will be done, on earth as it is in Heaven."

At one point, standing on the peak of the roof that extended from the centre, James burst into laughter and said, "You should see what is written here... 'Jesus land here'!" Of course, some of the other kids had to go and climb up to check it out. He was right!

Chapter 14 ~ Stones Laid Down...and Removed

We settled in after a night to remember. The boys slept at the "million star" hotel...on the roof.

The following day, we went to the Bridges for Peace Center and learned more about their work in bringing the Jewish people home from Siberia to Israel. They shared the concept that each act of kindness was helping to remove a stone in the way, making it possible for the Jewish people to respond positively to Christians after centuries of anti-Semitism, which had often been initiated by Christians. This reminded us of one of our mandates, "to remove the stones and prepare a highway."

> *Go through, go through the gates,*
> *Clear the way for the people;*
> *Build up, build up the highway,*
> *Remove the stones, lift up a standard over the peoples.*[77]

We were shown the distribution centre that operated to help supply the needs of the new Jewish immigrants. There we dropped off the extra shoes and toiletries that we had all brought with us to Israel, and thus, in a small way, we helped to "help bring the Jewish people home." Joshua took off his shoes and insisted on giving them to the cause, saying he had another pair back where we were staying.

At the King of Kings Community in Jerusalem we shared and presented in the evening service. After the service, a lady from the congregation had a prophetic word for us. She sensed that the message that we had brought would be the first of many other nations repenting for their anti-Semitism and helping with the return of the Jewish people.

~

Cradle Follow Up

Just before we left Israel to go back home, we returned to Arni and Yonit's place in Tel Aviv. There we prayed about what to do with the cradle. Should we leave it with them to share, or was there still something that the Lord wanted us to do with it back home? While we were in Jerusalem, David Demian called to encourage us and mentioned that there was going to be a meeting with the St Louis survivors in Ottawa the following November. After that call and the time of prayer we still didn't have a clear mandate, but we did think that, for now, we were to bring it back to Canada.

A few months after the time in Israel, I received this communiqué through Watchmen for the Nations:

> *Herbert Karliner, spokesman for the St. Louis survivors, arrived tonight. He is a gentle man with a sweet sense of humor considering what he has been through.*
>
> *Herbert's first words when he got off the plane tonight and met David were astounding. He had been reading the book, "None is Too Many" on the plane. As he read the part of the 1,000 kids he was shocked because he was one of the 1,000 children.*
>
> *Herbert had been taken as a young lad to an internment camp in France. It was from that camp*

Chapter 14 ~ Stones Laid Down...and Removed

that a request had been made to Canada to provide refuge for these children, but due to red tape had been denied! He had no idea at the time that there was a possibility that they were to go to Canada. All he knew was that he had to get away from there and so he ran and hid and was thus spared the fate of so many of his family and friends. Only he and his brother survived the Holocaust. His mother, father and two sisters never made it through the war years.

"God is doing an awesome thing", David said. "We have in our midst, a man who was not just rejected from Canada once - on the St. Louis ship, but twice - as one of the 1,000 children whose blood is on the hands of the Canadian government and a church that chose to keep silent rather than standing for righteousness."

To think that the King's Kids team of 24 young people and leaders had just returned from Israel where they identified with and repented for this very sin—the deaths of these 1,000 children. Now, today, God brings a surviving child that we didn't even know existed – into David and Rachel's home and into Canada to receive our repentance.[78]

~

The remaining survivors of the St. Louis were invited to Canada. The 25 survivors and their spouses who responded were brought to Ottawa at the expense of the Canadian church. Without any large corporate sponsorship, hundreds of thousands of dollars poured in from Canadian Christians throughout the nation. The survivors were flown in from Israel, Australia, England, the United States and Canada to Ottawa. They toured the

> city, including a visit to Parliament Hill and then they were hosted by 300 representatives of the Canadian church at the Friends of the St. Louis reception and dinner in Ottawa on November 5, 2000. At this reception, representatives of the Canadian church repented to the survivors for the Anti-Semitic acts of our nation.
>
> Among the many moving speeches and presentations during the night, perhaps none was as personally touching to the survivors as the presentation of a hand-crafted glass sculpture. After the date for this event had been set, it was discovered that the event was being held on the very day that Kristallnacht had occurred. This sculpture, designed particularly for this event, included a maple leaf base from which rise hands that are cradling a Star of David. Through the Star the St. Louis ship is emerging. The plaque with it states, 'Your people shall be my people and your God my God.'[79]

A part of the King's Kids team was able to share the dance to "When You Believe" that evening, and then they presented the story of the cradle. Rachel gave the prayer shawl to Herbert Karliner and placed it across his shoulders.

Something truly miraculous happened during this time in Ottawa. Healing and forgiveness replaced pain and bitterness, and deep bonds of trust, love and friendship were birthed between the St Louis survivors and the church of Canada.

After the "Journey to Jerusalem" and the subsequent meeting in Ottawa, we were overwhelmed at how the Lord had led the kids to be a part of what He

Chapter 14 ~ Stones Laid Down...and Removed

was doing in Canada. Besides desiring that the walls come down between the provinces and people groups, we were learning that His desire was that we would walk together as one in the church. What other stones needed to be removed? What other walls needed to come down?

Section Four

My prayer is not for them alone. I pray also for those who will believe in me through their message, that all of them may be one, Father, just as you are in me and I am in you. May they also be in us so THAT THE WORLD MAY BELIEVE *that you have sent me.*[80]

John 17:20–21 NIV

Chapter 15

Hand in Hand

GOD HAS AT times used kids in revivals, like in the Moravian revival and among the Huguenots, where even infants in their cribs were known to call cities to repentance. (Interestingly, many of the first settlers in Quebec were Huguenots.) More often, revival has started when one generation walked with the other. Josiah did not single-handedly turn his nation back to God. Even though he was king, he was humble enough to listen to the advice of those older and wiser than him. The same applied to Esther, who listened to Mordecai..."Who knows but that you have come to the kingdom for such a time as this and for this very occasion?"[81]

This is what is on God's heart. In Joel 1:3 God is speaking to the elders in the land: "Tell your sons about it, And let your sons tell their sons, And their sons the next generation. Then later on in Joel 2:28, "...I will pour out My spirit on all mankind; And your sons and daughters will prophesy, Your old men will dream dreams, Your young men will see visions."

Not one generation is left out. One of the things I learned at the Generation of Destiny seminar in the summer of '95 was the analogy of the arrow. Kids are like the tip of the arrow. They are strong, have an edge and provide impact. The adults are like the shaft that offers stability, but the grandparents are like the feathers that offer direction. The arrowhead would just fall straight down if launched on its own. With the shaft it would go a bit further, but it would not be able to stay on course and would miss the target. It takes all three working together to hit the target. This is a brilliant analogy, as at times we focus on one particular generation and exalt it, but God says He is the God of Abraham, Isaac and Jacob.

In the fall of 2001, we had the opportunity to spend a few months in Hawaii at the YWAM Kona base. We felt that one of the reasons the Lord led us there was to pray into the foundations of King's Kids. King's Kids had started there under the direction of Dale and Carol Kauffman about twenty-five years before. We learned the names of some local King's Kids staff and made several attempts to meet with them, but each time some unusual circumstance arose to prevent it. We began to sense that this was spiritual opposition. Finally, we managed to connect and were invited for supper. As we drove up to their home, a light rain began to fall and right above us a brilliant double rainbow bracketed their home. We stopped and marvelled at the sight. Over the next day, the Lord laid on our hearts to pray that God's purposes would not be aborted and that He would release a

Chapter 15 ~ Hand in Hand

fresh move of His Spirit, born out of water and fire, to break down the walls between the generations.

The next day, we were in a teaching session and the speaker shared how during the night the Lord had woken her up with the words "Water and Fire" and taken her into a deep time of prayer for a long time.

As she shared this, I was moved to intercede and the Lord gave me a vision of a volcano. On the top of the volcano there appeared to be sticks laid out like a nest and underneath was fire comprised of red, blue and yellow flames. But the "nest" didn't burn. As I watched, three golden eggs appeared in the nest. Eventually the eggs became translucent and children of all ages dressed in white started coming out of them. There was total silence. As I watched the scene unfolding, I noted that the earth around was exceedingly beautiful and clear. The trees were brilliant green and you could see each individual leaf and blade of grass. Then there came a sound of voices so loud and powerful that my ears literally burned. I couldn't hear what they were saying, but it was OH so wonderful. I wanted to join in with them because it was so beautiful, and yet when I did join, it was a heart-wrenching cry!

Then there was silence once again. After a period of time water came. It was like a huge wave, a Tsunami, but it was not a fearful wave. It covered us and we could breathe in it. The water was not of death, but of life. Then this, too, receded.

Then these words came, spoken with authority..."The Time has come, walls come down. Army, come forth, Pure Gold, born out of water and fire!" In my heart I knew it was partly referring to the walls between the generations.

As I reflected, I saw how God had been sharing His heart with both the younger and the older generations. We need one another. He is still the God of Abraham, Isaac and Jacob.

Later, I learned that in Kelowna, British Colombia, at a leadership Gathering that very week, they had felt led to each take a stick and then lay them down together in a bonfire as a symbol of unity.

~

On a Watchmen for the Nations video, David Demian shares how, a few years earlier, the Lord gave him a dramatic picture of His desire for English and French Canada. He was driving his car in Vancouver, and as his eyes wandered to the license plate of the car ahead of him, it suddenly changed. He saw interlocking wedding rings on one side and the words "I do" on the other. Tears came to his eyes so quickly that he had to pull over, and when he did, the Holy Spirit said, "David, this is my desire for English and French Canada. The day is coming when English Canada will realize they have been asking French Canada to do something that they themselves were unwilling to do: leave and cleave."

Many French Canadians perceive Canada as still tied to a British model. So to speak of unity is like asking them to marry English Canada and come live

Chapter 15 ~ Hand in Hand

at their in-laws' house. But marriage must be a leaving and cleaving for both parties.[82]

Remember what happened at boot camp before Mexico? Johnathan had a picture of a diamond engagement ring. It made no sense at all at the time, but in retrospect and in conjunction with the pictures of the walls coming down, it seemed to dovetail once again with what God was saying to other Christians in Canada. About this time it came to light that Sir John A. MacDonald, our first Prime Minister, referred to Confederation Day, July 1, 1867, by saying, "We are about to be united in Holy Matrimony…" Subsequent research has shown that the marriage analogy was commonly used by the fathers of Confederation in describing the formation of Canada.[83]

So, once again, we joined with the Watchmen team. That summer they were encouraging English Canadians to come to Quebec for what they called the Love Quebec tour. This was to encourage them to get to know and love the French people. While on the tour, we joined about 300 other French and English at the church in St. Eustache and had a time of worship together. Remember, this was the same church where, four years earlier, we had prayed that God would remove the hearts of stone and give the French and English a love for each other. New bonds of trust and unity had been built between the French and English to the point that our new Governor General, Michaëlle Jean, boldly declared: it is the end of the "Two Solitudes," referring to the book by Hugh Mac Lennan we had read.

Eight of the Quebec mission team members were present to witness this, but this time they were also able to meet and embrace Peg Byars and David Demian, who for all these years had faithfully arranged prayer covering over our projects.

A year or two later, we met in Quebec City at the "One Heart" Gathering, and there on stage was James, joining a God-initiated moment where the French, English and First Nations made covenant to walk together.

~

As God continues to lead and the walls are coming down, how do we transfer what we have learned about reconciliation and laying down our agendas on the national level to our homes and our cities? We look at the great commission and God's heart for the world. The kingdom of heaven is at hand—heal the sick, raise the dead, cleanse the lepers, cast out demons, freely you have received freely give—BUT wait till you are filled with power from on High, and you will be my witnesses from Jerusalem to Judea to the ends of the earth.

The disciples were instructed to wait for God's power to fill them, and they waited together in ONE ACCORD. They lay down their agendas and TOGETHER were willing to lay down their lives for each other. In this posture, God was able to come and fill them with power and authority such as they had not received before. Jesus had given them authority

Chapter 15 ~ Hand in Hand

before to heal the sick, and so on, while He was on earth, but this time the veil was removed from the eyes of those who witnessed these events, and 3,000 were added to the church in one day.

God still weeps at the hurts and injustice He sees. His agenda is still: "bring My sons from afar and my daughters from the ends of the earth"[84] WHY? "That they may KNOW Me and believe in Me...and be My witnesses." Whether they are prodigals that need to return from their drugs, alcoholism and rebellion, or the Jewish people returning to the Land of Israel, His cry is not only that they come home physically, but that they would KNOW Him and that they would turn around and let the world know—"I am HE that you seek..."—that His name would be hallowed and His glory rest among us.

In Revelation 4:2–3 it reads:

Immediately I was in the Spirit; and behold, a throne was standing in heaven, and One sitting on the throne. And He who was sitting was like a jasper stone and a sardius in appearance; AND THERE WAS A RAINBOW AROUND THE THRONE.[85]

In Ezekiel a similar picture is portrayed:

All around Him was a glowing halo, like a rainbow shining in the clouds on a rainy day. This is what the glory of the LORD looked like to me. (Ezekiel 1:28 NLT)

What is the connection between God's glory and the rainbow? Could it be His multifaceted nature, each colour expressing a part? A few months ago, I was in Edmonton helping lead a kids' track at a provincial gathering. During a time of prayer, a young boy had this prayer picture: He saw a church building covered with stripes of many colours, "like Joseph's rainbow coat." Behind the church was a big star, "like the morning star which is Jesus," and above it a golden cloud, "like the canopy of God's presence in the wilderness."

"When the church reaches out to the poor, hungry and hurting of the nations, God's presence will rest there," he concluded.

Along the same line, over the last year the Lord has impressed His heart for the poor and the homeless on the kids in our current Daniel Prayer Group. As a result, we have joined with a lady who works out of Bethlehem Aboriginal Church in the inner city, the same First Nations church that we talked about earlier. She hands out muffins once a week to street people and shares God's love with them. So the kids all made homemade muffins and off we went. One young girl said, "We didn't have chocolate chips at home so we put chocolate kisses in the muffins instead." As she went up to one girl who looked as though she worked the streets, she exclaimed, "Here is a muffin just for you. There is a chocolate kiss in it just to let you know that God loves you!" The girl received the muffin with tears in her eyes!

Chapter 15 ~ Hand in Hand

A short while later, another of the DPG boys saw a prayer picture of a church building that had all brick walls. In the middle was an angel with a pitchfork. The angel took it and broke it in half and then threw it into a caldron shaped like a muffin. Then he heard the word "JERICHO" and the walls of the building fell down. *When the church reaches out to the poor, like in the muffin ministry, the authority of the enemy is broken and the "walls" of the church fall down.*

Joseph's coat of many colours—the rainbow transferred to our level. It is God's heart of compassion, reconciliation, forgiveness and witness to families, the world and the Jewish people revealed. Remember, right at the start of this journey the Lord spoke to me and said, "Do not despise the day of small beginnings, for I will send a mighty downpour." God sends the rain to bring refreshing and to water the earth. "As the rays from the sun, My Son, hits the drops of rain; they cause My colours to be seen as I cleanse and remove hearts of stone."

Are we willing to lay down our agendas and our rights in order to come together as ONE and fulfill Jesus' prayer, "...that they may be one as the Father and I are one"?[86] Will we risk to dream again, to go outside our comfort zone, put on the rainbow coat and reach out to a world that is waiting to KNOW Him? Are we willing to be hinges that could turn around a generation and show them the truest form of Christianity, one that is filled with God's glory? As my son Shawn said, when they were speaking of world hunger in his grade one class, "Yes, Joseph fed the hungry, but there is a greater hunger, a spiritual hunger that God wants to fill as well." Let us ask God to give us His strategy to be His instruments to a hungry world.

~

The prophet Ezekiel clearly foretold the two steps that must always take place before any one of us can have the ability to cope with the evil in our world and receive power for service or witness. The first step is cleansing and consecration. "I (God) will sprinkle clean water on you and you will be clean. I will give you a new heart and put a new spirit within you." That is, through the Spirit, God will renew and refresh our attitudes, convict us of sin, begin to teach us about obedience and change our hearts. He will get us ready to be carriers of His glory. This is what the disciples went through while they walked with Jesus and while they waited in Jerusalem before Pentecost. The second step is that God will "Put His Spirit within us and cause us to walk in His ways."[87] This is what we long for—to be carriers of God's glory to the people of the nations, one by one by one. "Step by step, You'll lead me, and I will follow You all of my days."

Thinking about these things, I remembered a blond haired, three-year-old boy at the Edmonton Gathering. He took a hold of a golden pompom—the kind that cheerleaders use. It was one of the prayer tools we brought for the children. We had explained to the children before that gold was often seen as the colour of God's glory and that when they wanted to

Chapter 15 ~ Hand in Hand

pray for God's glory they could wave a golden streamer, flag or pompom. Well, here he was, at the front of the auditorium, pompom in hand and deliberately rubbing the sound system speakers and steps of the platform, up and down in a motion that looked like washing.

I went up to him and gently asked him what he was doing. "Washing," he replied.

I continued to observe him as he went on. Then I went up to him again and whispered, "Do you remember what Jesus washed?"

"Feet," he replied.

He looked up at me, and then at the people, and for the next thirty minutes he went and washed the feet of every single person there, all 250 of them, with his gold pompoms.

As I watched this, I remembered Jesus' example as HE washed the feet of His disciples before He commissioned them to go and serve a needy world. I wondered if that day our feet were being prepared to be carriers of His glory by a little child.

Epilogue

LOOKING BACK AT the kids that have been involved in the adventures that have been shared, I am thrilled that seven have continued on in Youth With A Mission and completed a Discipleship Training School. One even went to Quebec to do his DTS due to the impact of the 1998 Quebec mission trip. Six have entered or completed studies at various Bible colleges. Chuck left his job and entered into missions, planting radio receivers so the Gospel could be heard in remote areas of the world. Four have embarked on various missions, one actually spending eight months in Rwanda right after high school. James has continued to be involved with Watchmen for the Nations with a heart for the Aboriginal people. One of the girls is studying medicine with an eye towards missions. Naomi is involved with "Ballet Magnificat," while the "Nomi" from Israel is active with King's Kids in Israel. Dave and Rhonda are involved with welcoming newcomers to Canada. Carol and Erica continue to pour out their hearts for Israel. Doug's heart is stretched as the Lord leads him around the world: Rwanda, Taiwan, Russia, the Ukraine. Others have pursued studies with hopes of being a light in the marketplace. Still others are involved in reaching out to the inner city. Ruth is involved in prison ministry, but not before gentle Tuck passed away after a long struggle with cancer. Before he went to be with the Lord, they left a legacy of love for the Jewish people.

However, I am grieved that not all have stayed strong. Some, for a time, have been swept away, as they could not see a connection between what they saw on outreach and what they saw at school. They could see God's leading, but did not KNOW Him. They entered the world of low self-esteem and depression, "cutting" themselves to relieve the pain. A few fell into eating disorders and drug abuse when injustice was left seemingly unanswered.

Knowing about God is not the same as KNOWING God. I have struggled and wept as I have watched these kids wrestle. As Johnathan verbalized at the start, Jesus also weeps at their pain. Yet, I have seen God use the same struggles that they have gone through as springboards to give them a voice as they "love on" their peers with new understanding. In some instances they have crawled back into the Lord's embrace and embarked on careers through which they are able to seek to help others who struggle with what they themselves have gone through. Painful moments, as well as the awesome experiences we had on the journey, have been good teachers. We pray that God will draw the few that continue to struggle back to their first love, the love they embraced as children.

So what now? What are the next steps? We continue to pray that "step by step" He'll lead us. It has been an awesome privilege to follow His leading and to pray that God's glory fills our cities and nation. But how do we actually interface with and impact our society so that "the rubber hits the road," so to speak? How do we transfer the national vision and bring God's glory down to the people we connect with—at work, on our streets, at school? Do we have something to offer this generation as they struggle with eating disorders, low self-esteem and mind boggling temptations? How can we be God's instruments to help our friends really KNOW God so that their beliefs about God's love, God's mercy and His justice are strong enough that they won't be blown away by their feelings? How do we get to know God in all His glory so we won't be swept away when uncertainty and life's misfortunes cross our path?[88]

There is a great need to impact the children of the next generation so that they are able to own and articulate their faith, having a true heart knowledge that lasts instead of a "head" knowledge only, as was expressed at the Generation of Destiny seminar. They need to be able to transfer the "rainbow coloured liquid of God's glory poured out" to "the rainbow coloured coat walked out" and impact their world. Clarity of purpose and direction is essential for them to be like the sons of Issachar and understand the times they are living in. Instead of running away and hiding in our Christian groups, we need to leave the security of the "fold" and obey God's leading as His heart weeps over the pain in our streets. The very pain we have borne ourselves is part of the equipping that He will use and may be our point of connection to someone else's need.

Let us pray like Moses prayed: "Teach me your ways so I may know you."[89] As we embrace Him in greater intimacy and understand His ways, we will be able to stand and impact our society—and God's glory will fall.

Photo Gallery

*Celebration Tent in Atlanta, Target World.
The glory from the nations (Asia)
offered to the King.*

*Prayer tent at Target World.
Praying for walls to come down in Canada
with the Aboriginal peoples.*

*Serving an aboriginal community by literally
removing the walls—well, roof—of a church
on a reserve in Alberta as a first step to
bringing down the walls in our nation.*

Photo Gallery

*Praying "The Lord's Prayer"
at the Manitoba/Ontario border
en route to Montreal.*

Worship and heart preparation before outreach.

Section Four

Praying on Mount Royal at the observation site over the City of Montreal.

Praying for healing between the French and English people in Canada at L'Église Des Patriots with our hands touching the cannonball marks in the walls.

Photo Gallery

"Light Be"

*Shawn and the banner
at the front of St. Steven's Church.*

The cradle.

*Counting out the 1,000 grains of wheat;
100 grains per young person.*

Photo Gallery

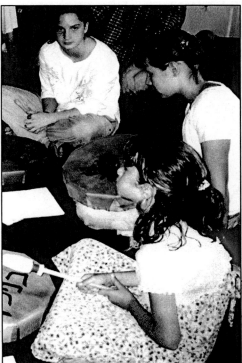

Using the drums with the names of the 12 tribes of Israel, we prayed for the continued fulfillment of God's promise for the return of the Jewish people to the Land of Israel according to the promises in Scripture.

Praying at the Western Wall.

(Note the prophetic team T-shirts.)

Section Four

Egypt and Israel walking together.
(Isaiah 19:23-25)

"God Sows"

Scattering seed in the valley of Jezreel in response to the prayer picture that two of the kids received there.

Photo Gallery

*Praying in the Jordan River:
Joshua, Rachel and David.*

*The stones from the
four corners of the earth.*

Section Four

Presentation of the cradle at the "Friends of the St. Louis" event in Ottawa.

The stones of remembrance from the Winnipeg Gathering.

Section Five

*Tell your sons about it,
And let your sons tell their sons,
And their sons the next generation.*

Joel 1:3

Activation

This is the confidence we have in approaching God: that if we ask anything according to his will, he hears us. And if we know that he hears us—whatever we ask—we know that we have what we asked of him.

1 John 5:14 NIV

A) Waiting on the Lord/ Hearing God's Voice

Materials needed:

- ☑ Bibles
- ☑ White board or static sheets
- ☑ Markers
- ☑ Worship music (either a worship CD or a worship leader familiar with songs of praise and adoration)

GOAL:
Both as individuals and as a group, to be able to discern what is on God's heart.

SETTING:
A comfortable room with worship music playing.

METHOD:
Using scriptural steps to prepare our hearts through worship, confession and waiting on God.

We are willing and ready to go, but where and what are we to do? How do we hear what is on God's heart? In her book, *Intercession, Thrilling and Fulfilling*,[90] Joy Dawson shares some steps that have been widely used as a guideline to hear what is on God's heart. In the work that we have done with King's Kids, God has given us incredible guidance this way. This is not the only way, but it is a helpful tool (pp. 74–78).

Principles for Effective Intercession:

Worship:

- Spend time in worship, praising God for who He is.
- Choose familiar hymns or choruses that focus on the character of God.
- Encourage people to speak out short prayers of praise and thanksgiving.

Confession:

- Read Psalm 139:23–24 (NIV)…*"Search me, O God, and know my heart; test me and know my anxious thoughts. See if there is any offensive way in me, and lead me in the way everlasting."* Pause and allow time for the Holy Spirit to convict of any unconfessed sin.
- Check carefully in relation to the sin of resentment and make sure that you have forgiven those who have wronged you (p. 75).

- Allow time for reconciliation in the group, if needed.
- Ask someone to lead in a prayer of confession.

E.g. "Lord, if I have done anything to make my hands dirty by doing things I should not have done, please forgive me and wash them to make them clean. We want to have clean hands and a pure heart like You talked about in the Bible."

Then we would ask the kids to put their hands on their hearts and pray,

"God, if my heart is not pure, make it pure right now. I want You to hear me when I pray. Forgive any bad thoughts I have had. AMEN!"

Acknowledge:

- ...that you can't really pray effectively without the Holy Spirit's help. (Romans 8:26b)
- Invite the Holy Spirit to fill you, guide you and control you as you pray. (Ephesians 5:18b)
- Pause and again deal with anything that the Lord may bring to mind that you need to repent of.
- Ask someone to lead in a prayer inviting the Holy Spirit's presence and guidance.

E.g. "Lord, You know all things, and we need the help of the Holy Spirit when we pray. What is on Your heart for today? What do You want us to pray for?"

Rebuke The Enemy:

- Read James 4:7 (NIV)..."*Submit yourselves, then, to God. Resist the devil, and he will flee from you.*"
- Have the leader come against any thoughts or intents of the enemy during this prayer time in the name of Jesus.

E.g. "Lord, we cover this place and all of us with the blood of Jesus. In the name of Jesus we say, 'Enemy, you have no place here and we don't invite you. You can't get a word in here!'"

Surrender:

- Your own imagination.
- Your wishes.
- Your burdens as to what you think you should pray for.
- Read Proverbs 3:5b..."*Do not lean on your own understanding.*"
- Read Isaiah 55:8a..."*For My thoughts are not your thoughts.*"

E.g. "Lord, we want You to take what we are thinking and worrying about right now. We want to give You our ideas about what we are to do on this outreach and we want to say 'thank You' that You want to talk to us like You talked to Samuel."

Praise God:

- TOGETHER Praise God and thank Him that He is a God who wants to speak with us.

Activation

Wait Silently

- Have your Bibles with you and respond to the Lord's promptings to passages in Scripture. (Psalm 62:5, Micah 7:7)
- He may also bring to mind a picture, a name of a person or a place.
- Allow 3-5 minutes for this. (Younger children often receive from the Lord much more quickly than older people.)

Gather Together

- On a white board or static sheet, record the thoughts that the group received from the Lord. It is important that everyone share his or her thoughts.
- Don't worry if what they receive doesn't make any sense. It may well be part of the puzzle and a necessary part of the bigger picture. It may also be something for a later time.
- Go over what you wrote down and see if there is a common theme or sense of direction.

Thank Him

- Thank God for the time with Him.
- Ask God for further confirmation.
- Take action on what God brings to mind in faith.[91]

Section Five

B) Putting on the "Rainbow Coat"[92]

Do you remember the prayer picture that the young boy received in Edmonton—a church with a rainbow coloured coat?

He was not the only one that had prayer pictures about "Joseph" and his rainbow coat that evening. God was really highlighting something. He was pointing out the importance of "the church" (not the building really, but the people that make up the church) reaching out.

Jesus' TOP priority was that we witness to the world out there (that is still held captive in the kingdom of darkness) in LOVING SERVICE. He asks us to draw close to Him in prayer so we know what is on His heart—after all, He sees the whole world—and then obey His promptings to reach out.

As we thought about it, we decided to explore the meanings behind the colours and use them as a springboard to "carry" God's glory out into the streets. So we designed a simple booklet and linked the various colours to a key of the kingdom. From there we wrote a simple prayer and a scripture fleshing out the principle.

Activation

We went over the booklet with the kids and suggested that for the next month they choose one of the colours each day as a reminder to bring that "key of the kingdom" into their world with God's help.

The kids were instructed to make a necklace out of rainbow coloured beads or to place a single bead on a fine wire that they could tie onto a necklace or bracelet they were wearing already. Another option was to encourage them to wear an item of clothing reflecting the colour that they were going to choose for the day.

As I am writing this, I received an email from Toni. She shared,

> *As I left Cuba, where we were vacationing, I saw "rainbow beams" coming from the sky to the top of the wing of the plane with colors of pink, blue, yellow, turquoise and mauve. The beams, however, did not land on the ground. There was cloud cover for the remainder of the flight but as soon as the plane flew over Toronto the sky was bright and I again saw "rainbow beams," this time coming from below the clouds and landing on the ground. There were also circular patches of colors on the ground, similar colors to the above.*[93]

Isn't that neat? I was actually on a plane going to Seattle and saw the exact same thing a short while later! So let's get on with it and be a witness in our actions and our words to testify to God's love.

Section Five

1) Key Colours

Materials:
- ☑ Colourful Beads
- ☑ Elastic, wire or fishing line to string beads on
- ☑ Colour booklet printed out, one per child
- ☑ Pencil crayons

Optional
- ☑ Rainbow parachute
- ☑ Cookies with coloured Smarties for snack
- ☑ Copy of the song by Avalon, "Testify to Love"

GOAL:
To help kids intentionally carry kingdom principles into the world.

SETTING:
Room large enough to do crafts and a parachute game.

Red

Key of the Kingdom: Love

"For God so loved the world that he gave his one and only Son, that whoever believes in him shall not perish but have eternal life." John 3:16 NIV

> *Lord, help me to know how much You love me. Help me to show Your love to someone today in simple acts of kindness. Open my eyes to see the need in the people You bring across my path today. Give me Your love for them and the strategy that would touch their hearts.*

Orange

Key of the Kingdom: Courage

(THE FIRE OF THE HOLY SPIRIT)

"Be strong and courageous! Do not tremble or be dismayed, for the Lord your God is with you wherever you go." Joshua 1:9

> *Lord, I need courage today. You know how I face temptations to do wrong every day. Help me to be like Shadrach, Meshach and Abednego, who stood up for You and didn't follow the crowd, even when it was very hard. Help me to resist temptation. Thank You that You promise to be with me everywhere I go. (see Daniel 3:28)*

Yellow/Gold

Key of the Kingdom: Truth

(JESUS; THE LIGHT OF THE WORLD!)

"By day the Lord went ahead of them in a pillar of cloud to guide them on their way and by night in a pillar of fire to give them light." Exodus 13:21 (NIV)

> *Show me that You are with me today. Be my guide, and help me know Your truth in the circumstances I face during the day. Help me to be a child of Light and bring Your light into my world.*

Green

Keys of the Kingdom:
Life, hope, healing, and new beginnings

"...I came that they may have and enjoy life, and have it in abundance (to the full, till it overflows)." John 10:10 (AMP)

Lord, open my eyes to someone who needs a word of life or hope today. Give me Your words or acts to bring healing into his/her life.

Light Blue

Key of the Kingdom: Peace

(THE WATER OF THE HOLY SPIRIT)

"Don't fret or worry. Instead of worrying, pray. Let petitions and praises shape your worries into prayers, letting God know your concerns. Before you know it, a sense of God's wholeness [GOD'S PEACE], everything coming together for good, will come and settle you down." Philippians 4:6–7 (MESSAGE)

Today when I am worried, help me to remember that You are in control. When I run into situations today where there is there is conflict or hurting, help me to bring Your peace into the problem.

Indigo/Dark Blue

Key of the Kingdom: Obedience

(HEARING GOD'S VOICE)

"...mark each corner tassel [of your prayer shawl] with a blue thread. When you look at these tassels you'll remember and keep all the commandments of God, and not get distracted by everything you feel or see..." Numbers 15:38–41 (MESSAGE)

"When ye pray, say, Our Father which art in heaven, Hallowed be thy name. Thy kingdom come. Thy will be done, as in heaven, so in earth." Luke 11:2 (KJV)

> *Lord, help me listen to Your still small voice and obey. Help me to obey Your still small voice even when it doesn't make sense. Use me today to do Your will on Earth as it is in Heaven. Use my hands, my mouth and my feet to bring Your compassion, kindness and truth into my world.*

Violet/Purple

Key of the Kingdom: Authority

"Then Jesus came to them and said, 'All authority in heaven and on earth has been given to me. Therefore go and make disciples of all nations, baptizing them in the name of the Father and of the Son and of the Holy Spirit, and teaching them to obey everything I have commanded you. And surely I am with you always, to the very end of the age.'" Matthew 28:18–20 (NIV)

> *Thank You that You have authority over the kingdom of darkness and that You have given that authority to me. Jesus, use my voice to speak out the words of truth and blessing that You would want to say. Use me to draw someone to You today.*

Pink

Key of the Kingdom: Good relationships, Unity

"I [Jesus] pray also for those who will believe in me through their message, that all of them may be one, Father, just as you are in me and I am in you. May they also be in us so that the world may believe that you have sent me." John 17:20–21 (NIV)

The goal is for all of us to become one heart and mind!

> *Jesus, help me today to be like You. Show me how to get along with_____ so that others will know that You are in me and believe in You.*

White

Key of the Kingdom: Purity

"Finally, brothers, whatever is true, whatever is noble, whatever is right, whatever is pure, whatever is lovely, whatever is admirable—if anything is excellent or praiseworthy—think about such things." Philippians 4:8 (NIV)

"...become blameless and pure, children of God without fault in a crooked and depraved generation, in which you shine like stars in the universe." Philippians 2:15 (NIV)

> *If I am in a situation where I am tempted today, help me to choose to think about the things that will bring joy to Your heart. Help me to walk as a child of Light.*

Black

Key of the Kingdom: Humility

(DEATH TO SELF & SIN)

"The lifestyle of the wicked is like total darkness, and they will never know what makes them stumble." Proverbs 4:19 (CEV)[94]

Activation

"...If your first concern is to look after yourself, you'll never find yourself. But if you forget about yourself and look to me, you'll find both yourself and me." Matthew 10:38–39 (MESSAGE)

Help me to see others through Your eyes, Jesus. Help me to remember that Your ways are better than my ways and to not insist on having my way. When I feel like being selfish, help me to remember that You gave Yourself for us.

2) Parachute Games

Purpose:

1.) Visualize a canopy, like Gods' glory over a person or a nation.

2.) Pray for a person or nation, using the colour principles.

   a. Review **basic guidelines** re: using a parachute. (See website listed below.)

   b. Place a map of your nation on the floor, or chose one of the participants to sit in the middle of the floor.

   c. Cover the map or person with the parachute, and instruct the rest of the kids to hold the edges of the parachute by the handles

"Canopy"

- Players lower the parachute and then on the count of three raise their arms high. Once the parachute is quite high, everyone then quickly takes three or four giant steps toward the center and pulls the parachute behind them, sitting down with their bottoms on the edge of the parachute.

- Being in the *Canopy* brings a sense of peace, calm and wonder. Discuss: being in the "canopy" is like being in a safe. peaceful "God Place" together.
- Encourage prayer for the nation or person under the canopy, using the thoughts that were learned from the colours booklet.
- E.g., Help _____ to show God's love today. Give the leaders in our nation of _____ to have the courage to speak the truth... and so on.

"Putting On the Rainbow Coat"

- Have one of the children sit in the middle of the parachute and the rest hold the handles.
- All together pray that "Johnny" will be a carrier of God's glory this week.
- Slowly walk in the same direction, "wrapping" the parachute around the child (make sure it doesn't go as far as their neck).
- When they are "wrapped" in the coat, have the kids holding the handles on a count of three pull and take a large step backwards.
- The child in the center will spin...

For information regarding parachute activities:
http://www.funandgames.org/parachute_games.html

Postscript

ON THE NATIONAL level, as Renee said ten years ago, "God seems to be working really fast in accord with us." Even while this book has been at the publishers, on May 14, 2008, the Canadian Jewish Congress wrote a letter commending the Canadian government for creating an educational program with plans to build a memorial commemorating the Jewish refugees of the St. Louis Ship.

> "We are grateful that the Canadian government and the Honourable Jason Kenney, the Secretary of State for Multiculturalism in particular, have recognized this dreadful time in Canadian history," said Sylvain Abitbol co-president of Canadian Jewish Congress. "The curse of anti-Semitism has never been more evident in a Canadian context than with the plight of the Jews of the ship St. Louis."[95]

Then June 11, 2008, was another historic day for Canada as our Prime Minister, Steven Harper, along with the leaders of the opposition parties, apologized to and asked forgiveness of our First Nations People for the abuses brought to them through our previous governments' policies, attitudes and implementation of residential schools. As we listened intently, we heard what we have prayed and longed to hear for many years and wept with thanksgiving to God for moving upon our government leaders in this way. We wept as we heard many of our Aboriginal people say, "Now the healing can begin."

Isn't it amazing? Or should I say, "Isn't HE amazing?!"

Endnotes

1. "Sometimes By Step," words and music by Rich Mullins and Beaker © 1991, 1992 Edward Grant, Inc. (ASCAP)/Kid Brothers of St. Frank Publishing (ASCAP).

2. King's Kids, Generation Of Destiny Seminar, Russell Sanche speaker. July 2005, Trinity Baptist Church, Winnipeg, MB.

3. Chuck Pierce/White Dove Ministries, *The Shepherd's Rod 2008*, www.whitedoveministries.org (accessed Jan 15, 2008), p. 2.

4. Ibid., p. 1.

5. Mark 10:14 NIV

6. 1 Corinthians 12: 12-27

7. Solders with little Feet weekend, Dian Layton speaking. Spring 2006, Trinity Baptist Church, Winnipeg, MB.

8. Esther Ilinsky, "Do Not hinder the Children," *Christian Week*, Fall 1995.

9. Isaiah 43:5-13 NIV

10. 1 Samuel 3:10

11. "Let Your Glory Fall," words and music by David Ruis © 1992 Mercy Publishing, 5409 Maryland Way, Ste. 200 Brentwood, TN 37027.

12. Verses 6-9 are quoted from NASB, but verse 10a is quoted from NLT.

13. Evening Bulletin for Celebration Tent, Day Two, Target World, 1996. (Prepared by the Global Kings' Kids team.)

14. Evening Bulletin for Celebration Tent, Day Five, Target World, 1996. (Prepared by the Global Kings' Kids team.)

Section Five

---

[15] "Ancient of Days," words and music by Gary Sadler and Jamie Harvill (C) 1992 Integrity's Hosanna! Music/ASCAP & Integrity's Praise! Music/BMI c/o Integrity Media, Inc., 1000 Cody Road, Mobile, Al 36695. All Rights Reserved. International Copyright Secured. Used by Permission.

[16] Todd Rutkowski, Target World '96 Outreach Director.

[17] Bulletin for Celebration tent, Commissioning, Target World, 1996. (Prepared by Global King's Kids team.)

[18] "Foundations, destiny and calling," *King's Kids Manual*, p. 20.

[19] "Above All Else," words and music by Kirk and Deby Dearman © 1988 Integrity's Hosanna! Music/ASCAP & Integrity's Praise! Music/BMI c/o Integrity Media, Inc., 1000 Cody Road, Mobile, Al 36695. All Rights Reserved. International Copyright Secured.

[20] E-mail from Canada in Prayer, March 4, 1998.

[21] Ibid.

[22] Ezekiel 36:25–26

[23] Allan Heron, "Montreal and Area YFC," *Vision*, Issue 8, Easter 2002, p. 2.

[24] Faytene C. Kryskow, *Stand on Guard* (Credo Publishing, 2005) p.89.

[25] 2 Chronicles 7:14 (NIV)

[26] Prayer prayed while on "Its a new Day" program # 23273.

[27] "The Lord is Come," words and music by Ric Marchi, © 1987 ZionSong music (P.O. Box 574044 Orlando, FL 32857).

[28] Joshua 1:13

[29] Isaiah 52:7 NIV

[30] "Children of Light," words and music by Andy Park, Copyright © 1991 Mercy Publishing, 5409 Maryland Way,

Endnotes

Ste. 200 Brentwood, TN 37027. All rights reserved. International copyright secured.

31 Mathew 5:16

32 "Shout to the North," words and Music by Martin Smith, © 1995 Curious? Music U.K. (admin. by EMI Christian Music Publishing). All rights reserved. International copyright secured.

33 "No Higher Calling," words and music by Lenny Leblanc and Greg Gulley © 1989,1999 Doulos Publishing (Maranatha! Music [Admin. by The Copyright Company]) All rights reserved. International copyright secured.

34 "St-Eustache et les patriots" accessed February 8, 2008 at http://daoust53.homestead.com/StEustachePmonuments.html.

35 "Rise Up," words and music by Dale Garratt and Trevor Yaxley © 1989 Scripture in Song/Maranatha Music, (administered by Music Services, www.musicservices.org) ASCAP. All rights reserved. Used with permission.

36 Watchmen for the Nations, "The Journey" (online article accessed February 6, 2008 at www.watchmen.org). Quoted with permission by David Demian, March 17, 2008.

37 Erving Abella and Harold Tropper, *None Is Too Many: Canada and the Jews of Europe 1933-1948* (Toronto: Key Porter Books, 2002).

38 E-mail update on the Train of Intercession from Peg Byars, February 25, 1999.

39 Daniel 9:3–5

40 Watchmen for the Nations, "The Journey" (online article accessed February 6, 2008 at www.watchmen.org). Quoted with permission by David Demian, March 17, 2008.

41 Joel 2:15–16

42 Psalm 51:17

[43] Watchmen for the Nations, "The Journey" (online article accessed February 6, 2008 at www.watchmen.org). Quoted with permission by David Demian, March 17, 2008.

[44] Genesis 9:13–15 (author's emphasis in caps)

[45] Isaiah 43:5–8, 10 NIV

[46] Erving Abella and Harold Tropper, *None Is Too Many: Canada and the Jews of Europe 1933-1948* (Toronto: Key Porter Books, 2002).

[47] Author's emphasis indicated by italics.

[48] Isaiah 62:4

[49] Ellen Gunderson Traylor, *Jerusalem: The City of God* (Eugene, OR: Harvest House, 1995) p. 625.

[50] Numbers 3:6–17

[51] Ruth 1:16 NIV

[52] Matthew 2:18

[53] Mathew 2:18 NIV

[54] Jeremiah 39:2

[55] Isaiah 62:10

[56] "I Know Your Name," words and music by Beverly Darnall and Michael W. Smith © 1998 Annie Merie Music, Sony/ATV Milene Music.

[57] United States Holocaust Memorial Museum, Washington, D.C. "Kristallnacht" Holocaust Encyclopedia Last Updated: October 25, 2007, www.ushmm.org (accessed February 5, 2008).

[58] "When You Believe" from *The Prince of Egypt* motion picture. Words and Music by Stephen Schwartz Copyright (c) 1997 DWA Songs (ASCAP) Worldwide Rights for DWA Songs Administered by Cherry Lane Music Publishing Company, Inc. International Copyright Secured. All Rights Reserved. Used by permission.

Endnotes

59 "Hashivenu," Israeli Folk song, author unknown. Arrangement by Sally K. Albrecht. (Public Domain)

60 Lamentations 5:21

61 Numbers 6:24–26

62 Isaiah 40:1

63 Ezekiel 11:17–20

64 Ezekiel 37:17

65 "Watchmen," words and music by Russ Rosen © 1996 Arrows in the Hand Music, Administrated by Big Tree Publishing, Box 281, Fort Langley, B.C. Canada. All rights reserved. Used with permission.

66 1 Samuel 3:9

67 1 Kings 18:21

68 Psalm 72:8 KJV

69 Jeremiah 24:6–7

70 E-mail from Chuck Kim, August 2000.

71 Isaiah 60:9b

72 Revelation 22:2 NIV

73 Joshua 3:5

74 Adapted from the song "Here By the Water" Music and lyrics by Jim Croegaert © 1993 Rough Stones Music.

75 Isaiah 35:1–2

76 *In Defense of Israel*, John Hagee, Front Line, Lake Mary, Florida, pg 13, (c) 2007 Thomas Nelson Publishers.

77 Isaiah 62:10

78 E-mail communication from Watchmen for the Nations, October 2000.

79 Watchmen for the Nations, "The Journey" (online article accessed February 6, 2008 at www.watchmen.org). Quoted with permission.

Section Five

80 Author's emphasis in caps.

81 Esther 4:14 AMP

82 Watchmen for the Nations, "The Journey" (online article accessed February 6, 2008 at www.watchmen.org). Quoted with permission.

83 Ibid.

84 Isaiah 43:6 NIV

85 Author's emphasis in caps.

86 See John 17:22.

87 Catherine Marshall, *The Helper*, (Waco, TX: Word Books, 1978) pp. 38-39.

88 Randall Arthur, *Wisdom Hunter* (Sisters, OR: Questar Publishers, Inc., 1991) p. 237.

89 Exodus 33:13 NIV

90 Joy Dawson. *Intercession: Thrilling and Fulfilling* (Seattle: YWAM Publishing, 1997).

91 Adapted from Carolin Sadler, *Warrior Bride Arise* (Belleville, ON: Essence Publishing, 2004) pp. 197-200.

92 ideas for this activation from Ester Wogburg, Lezlie Martinson and Carolin Sadler.

93 E-mail from Toni Severn, February 19, 2008.

94 Scripture marked as "CEV" taken from the Contemporary English Version Copyright © 1995 by American Bible Society. Used by permission.

95 E-mail from Jason Kenny, M.P., May 14, 2008. Quoting from a letter by Jordan Kerbel, National Director of Public Affairs, Canadian Jewish Congress.

Has your heart connected with *The Journey*?

Check out:

Kids of the King, Arise!
www.kidsofthekingarise.blog.com

YWAM/King's Kids Winnipeg:
www.ywamkkwinnipeg.com

Watchmen for the Nations:
www.watchmen.org

Books by Carolin Sadler...

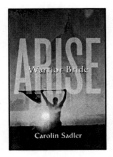

Warrior Bride Arise
by Carolin Sadler

"Through *Warrior Bride Arise*, Carolin has stepped forward to declare the value, and even the criticalness of children, preteens and teens to rise up and take their place among the warriors of this era of Christendom. Carolin writes with passion and practicality in giving the tools to see kids prepared and readied for a life of total devotion. Hear her heart shout, 'Arise!' and allow your children to respond to the heart of God."

~***Russell. J Sanche***
KKI National Director
Youth With A Mission

Also by Carolin Sadler...

The Blessing

by Carolin Sadler/Illustrated by Rosalind Amorin

This book explores God's desire for us to enter into His rest. Written for young children the Sabbath rest is looked at, by observing a Jewish Shabbat. As the family in the story interacts an age old blessing is pronounced.

In our frantic society and family disintegration scripture offers a foundation to restore the hearts of the Fathers to the children, and the children to the fathers. The activities at the end of the book are geared to help the whole family experience God's rest, presence and blessing.

Available in French and English (la benediction)

On Daddy's Knees

by Carolin Sadler/Illustrated by Rosalind Amorin

This interactive story book is a first look at hearing God's voice, journaling, and evangelism for the younger child.

> "It was so sweet to my heart to come closer to Jesus through this story. Thank you so much for your heart and may the children find rest in Jesus."
>
> ~***Alain Caron***
> *French Pastor & leader with*
> *Watchmen for the Nations.*

Available in English & French (Sur Les Genoux de Jesus)

Printed in the United States
118271LV00008B/3/P